"Although pastors may have talked among themselves about how to construct effective sermons, they have seldom brought the listeners into the conversation. After all, what could laypeople contribute to the discussion? Meirwyn Walters is uniquely qualified to make such a contribution to pastors who preach Sunday after Sunday. He grew up in a preacher's family, has been an active member of several congregations, and has heard his share of mediocre sermons. He has also listened to sermons that God used to bring his people into a deeper, fuller relationship with himself. He has thought a great deal about the difference."

—Haddon Robinson (1931–2017)
Harold John Ockenga Distinguished Professor of Preaching
Gordon-Conwell Theological Seminary

"A lot of books have been written about preaching by those who spend their time standing behind a pulpit. Few, if any, have been written about preaching by those who occupy the pew. Meirwyn Walters is uniquely qualified for such a task, and he "brings it" in his book *Intentional Preaching*. If you're a preacher like Meirwyn's legendary father, read this book and consider his practical advice and conceptual reflections as a handbook to strengthen your sermons. If you're a pew-sitter like Meirwyn, then ponder his thoughts on how to listen better and grow more through the weekly homily you receive. I know Meirwyn as a dear friend, and his observations are not only insightful, but the heart of this author wants nothing less than to build up the church. A must-read for all churchgoers and church leaders."

—Barry H. Corey, President of Biola University;
author of *Love Kindness: Discover the Power of a Forgotten Christian Virtue*

"Preaching is more, but not less, than making a good argument from a text. What better feedback from the faithful can we get than that which is shaped by years of legal training and experience—not to mention, growing up with a seasoned preacher! Meirwyn Walters's reflections here reward not only us preachers but our hearers. I heartily recommend this book!"

—Michael Horton
J. Gresham Machen Professor of
Systematic Theology and Apologetics
Westminster Seminary California

"This is the book I've been waiting forty years to read. Each Sunday when I rise up to preach, I find myself wondering what my people are expecting of me. Saccharine comments following a worship service ("Nice sermon, pastor") are pleasant but not helpful. At last, a knowledgeable layman has written on behalf of his fellow pew-sitters an extremely helpful and practical compendium of wisdom and counsel directed to us preachers. As one who had the privilege of being taught in a seminary preaching class by his father, Gwyn Walters (one of the truly great twentieth-century preachers), I am thrilled to see that so much of his father lives in him and in this book."

—Doug Pratt, Senior Pastor, First Presbyterian Church
Bonita Springs, Florida

"Meirwyn Walters's view from the pew is a rich, informative perspective about which any preacher wants to be aware. His insights and advice will help preachers make thoughtful decisions about the task of preaching. Every preacher would be benefited by reading this enjoyable, well-written, and insightful book!"

—Scott M. Gibson, Professor of Preaching
The David E. Garland Chair of Preaching
George W. Truett Seminary, Baylor University

"This little book is a creative and convicting read that made me chuckle and check my own preaching. Written in bite-sized chunks that cover an array of subjects from alliteration, application, authenticity, to 'ahhs,' this little volume will help you grow as a preacher. But this is no random 'view from the pew'; rather, it is the laser-focused vision of a man who has sat under one of the great preachers: his father and teacher of preachers, Gwyn Walters. It is also the view of a man who preaches himself, and who knows the trials and temptations the preacher faces. Well worth reading and heeding."

—Jonathan Thomas
Pastoral Dean of Union School of Theology, UK
Pastor of Cornerstone Church, Abergavenny, Wales

"Rarely does anyone evaluate preaching from a layperson's perspective, even though the laity are the target audience of nearly all sermons. From a wealth of experience as a committed Christian, father, husband, church leader, and also son of a Welsh pastor and preaching professor, Meirwyn Walters engagingly addresses modern preachers. He provides practical advice in a clear and clever way to help preachers understand how a layperson listens. *Intentional Preaching* reads easily, contains many memorable and heartwarming stories, and delivers sensible and practical advice. Even if one has delivered sermons for many years, *Intentional Preaching* will help pastors and laypeople from many different backgrounds think more critically about the great craft and tough job of delivering sermons to modern audiences."

—H. Drake Williams, III, Associate Professor of New Testament
Evangelische Theologische Faculteit, Leuven, Belgium;
Minister of Mission and Theology
Central Schwenkfelder Church, Lansdale, Pennsylvania

"*Intentional Preaching* is unique in perspective, practical in content, and inspiring in personal reflection—belying its claim to be a mere collection of 'bits and bobs of advice.' Meirwyn will not only convince you that intentional preaching is the key to good preaching but will also show you how. Most powerfully, he dwells on the preacher's hardest tasks—illustrating and applying—by illustrating and applying throughout the book."

—Elizabeth E. Shively
Senior Lecturer in New Testament Studies
St. Mary's College, University of St. Andrews

"This is a gem of a book chock-full of applicable insights you will not find in other preaching books. Even a few minutes spent reading this book amidst a pastor's busy week is guaranteed to strengthen that week's sermon. Walters's work is winsome, passionate, and relentlessly practical, and I recommend it to everyone who wants to be a better preacher."

—Nelson E. Ould, Lead Pastor
Community West Church, Henrico, Virginia

"Books on preaching are numerous. Helpful books on preaching more rare. This is one of those more rare volumes. I don't agree with every conclusion in these pages, but I agree with almost every conclusion! While the author is professionally a lawyer, his father was a preacher and a teacher of preachers (he taught me). Now, joining the experience of learning from his father and listening for himself, Walters presents us with a wonderful mix of edification and enjoyment. Reading this as a father, I can scarcely conceive of a more moving tribute from a son."

—Mark Dever, Pastor
Capitol Hill Baptist Church, Washington DC

"If you ever preach, but somehow miss this excellent book on how to do so better, the dull stares of congregations may haunt you for decades to come! You have been warned. Incidentally, this is just the book to prevent that from happening! Seriously."

—Eric Metaxas
New York Times* best-selling author of *Martin Luther
Host of the nationally syndicated *Eric Metaxas Radio Show*

Intentional Preaching

Intentional Preaching

Meirwyn Walters

HENDRICKSON PUBLISHERS

Intentional Preaching: A View from the Pew

Hendrickson Publishers Marketing, LLC
P. O. Box 3473
Peabody, Massachusetts 01961-3473
www.hendrickson.com

ISBN 978-1-68307-268-3

Printed in the United States of America

First Printing — March 2020

Library of Congress Control Number: 2020931278

To my father, Gwyn Walters.
In person, a short, humble, and quiet Welshman;
but in the pulpit, immense.

Gwyn Walters preaching on the shore of the Sea of Galilee (c. 1989).

Contents

Foreword

The author of this insightful book—my friend Meirwyn Walters—is the son of a preacher who also taught preachers how to preach. Some preachers' children would do anything to avoid listening to sermons. Instead, this preacher's kid has written a book that provides wise advice for any preacher to follow. Walters's perspective is from the pew. He speaks as a thoughtful and informed listener to matters that many preachers overlook or even ignore.

Born into the home of a preacher and professor of preaching, Walters is not unfamiliar with listening to sermons. He was schooled informally and formally about the task of preaching. As a child, he was regularly given the challenge by his professor father to put together short sermons while the family sat at the dinner table. The family feasted on preaching! Years later, Walters engaged in formal theological studies before heading to law school, where he put into practice pulpit oratory skills arguing cases before juries and judges—and with skill and insight he continues to do so today. As an elder in the church of which he's a member, Walters occasionally preaches, as well as cheers his home church pastors and other preachers with winsome words of encouragement.

This encouraging approach to preaching appears to have been inspired by Meirwyn Walters's upbringing. I'm a beneficiary of the immeasurable encouragement that radiated from his father, Dr. Gwyn Walters. When I was a young, inexperienced student interested in preaching, Dr. Walters stood by me and nurtured me in the task of preaching. He then supported me in the next step of further study in the field of preaching. He was there when I served as a pastor and even opened the way for me to teach preaching, which has been my calling and career. Meirwyn Walters comes by this task of encouraging preachers naturally, even spiritually.

I am pleased to commend this book to readers, because I'm confident you will benefit from reading it. Walters understands the plight of preachers. Preaching is tough work. He knows about the distractions and frustrations of pastoral ministry. And he knows what listeners need—they don't need a preacher's scraps; they need a nourishing feast, a feast from God's word that will strengthen them as they face their fractured families, belligerent bosses, complaining customers, or screaming school children.

Walters is aiming at helping preachers bring their A++ game into the pulpit every week. The time that a preacher spends in the pulpit is to be intentional, notes Walters. In every helpful chapter of this book, Walters argues that "the key to good preaching is to make each of your decisions deliberately, consciously, intentionally, with the goal of communicating with the greatest effectiveness." He assists us as readers to reflect on everything we do as we preach, in order for us to become better at the preaching task. From what preachers wear to how preachers conduct themselves, Walters provides words of encouragement and instruction in the chapters that follow.

Although Meirwyn Walters calls himself "just a guy in the pew," this "guy" gives great advice on how we as preachers can become better at what we do. As disciples of Jesus Christ, we're always learners—that's what the word *disciple* means. If that's the case, then read this book as a learner, ready to develop and grow as a preacher. You may be a young learner or an older one like me. Either way, you will be shaped by the insights from this "guy in the pew" who wants nothing more than to help you become the preacher God has called you to be. I know, because I'm all the better for having read this book.

Scott M. Gibson
Professor of Preaching
The David E. Garland Chair of Preaching
George W. Truett Seminary
Baylor University

Acknowledgments

To every preacher I've ever heard, you have contributed to the substance of this book. Whether your sermon was a paragon of emulation or at times a bit of a cautionary tale, I admire each of you for taking on this most important of endeavors in exhorting us from God's word. My walk with the Lord has been and continues to be greatly formed by your hard and loving work.

Haddon Robinson remarkably agreed to read the manuscript twice. The differences between what he read initially and what you hold in your hand were in great part the result of his perceptive and kindly comments.

To each of those whose endorsements appear in the book, I am deeply humbled: that you would take time away from your far more important duties to read it and then for the kind commendations you provided.

To Patricia Anders, I am exceedingly grateful for your willingness to imagine the worth of a layman's view on preaching and for your shepherding of this project, along with your expert editorial suggestions and painstaking review of the manuscript.

To my sister, Gwenfair Adams, you provided invaluable comments on the drafts and kept pushing me. As with most intellectual pursuits, you beat me and got published first (twice over). You're the best "big sister" a brother could have, and your input and support for this book provide no exception.

To my mother, Mair, dotting the manuscript with little red-penned checkmarks was the least of your contributions to this book. Your deep devotion to your preacher husband and your lifelong striving to create the context from which he could go each Sunday to preach, free from distractions, underscored to me the profound importance of his pulpit work. To this day, your sacrifices as a "preacher's wife" continue to pay extraordinary dividends in the lives of those who sat under your husband's preaching.

To my son, David Gwyn, and daughters, Mari Elizabeth and Carys Reese, you have put up with your father's household preaching admirably. May you find in these pages a deep sense of why, for the rest of your lives, getting yourselves to church every Sunday morning to hear what God has to say to you will be the most highly leveraged hour of your week.

How does one thank one's father? From him I learned the art and science of preaching, for as his son I watched his every move. He began every sermon on his knees in his study and finished it in the pulpit pointing us all heavenward. What those outside saw was what he was within the walls of our home. How I would have enjoyed presenting him with the first copy of this little tome. He was and remains my only earthly hero; I have needed no other.

I must hasten to say that it is quite likely that he would not have agreed with everything in this book. And while he heard thousands of sermons in his capacity as a professor of homiletics, very seldom did he—unlike me—sit in a church on Sunday listening to someone else preach. Thus I must take the blame for anything amiss in this book. One of my pastors used to ask, "Any questions, comments, or indignant refutations?" It is the latter for which I take full responsibility.

And, finally, to my dearest Nina. With your encouragement, humor, and unwavering affection, you have been my muse. Your passion for all things church, your theological perspicacity, and your keen insights into the place of the pulpit in our lives as a family have enriched me beyond measure and have found their place in this book.

To you, our Heavenly Father—the inspiration, reason, object, substance, and point of every sermon—may you be glorified by whatever these pages prompt and produce.

It's a Tough Job

Ever spent a day shaving pigs? Apparently that's a job for some people. It makes the pig's muscles stand out so the hope for future bacon looks brighter. Ever worked as an oil tank removal technician? A sinkhole garbage specialist, concrete-wall demolisher, or slime eel fisher?

Ever collected owl pellets? Owls swoop down on a rodent, gulp it down, digest it, and then regurgitate the remaining bones and fur in a tidy little package. It seems that there's a market for the stuff in educational institutions across America, where students and professors analyze it with gusto. And someone has to go out into the woods to gather it.

Mike Rowe made quite a career trying out these and other remarkably dirty, even hazardous jobs, starring in a Discovery Channel show aptly called *Dirty Jobs*. During the run of the show, he dabbled in more than three hundred tough jobs.

One day, he should try preaching!

If you are a preacher, you have one of the more demanding jobs around. Assuming you are fortunate, you "only" have to get into the pulpit forty-eight Sundays a year. (The other four are probably spent visiting your in-laws.) Rain or shine, you've simply got to show up and, feel like it or not, you've got to preach.

If you are unforgivably organized, you get twelve to fifteen hours a week to prepare your sermon. This is assuming that dear old Mrs. McGillicutty doesn't head heavenward this week, that your adult Sunday school teacher didn't just have a baby, and that the regional district of your denomination is not having its annual chicken dinner. But, of course, one of those things is happening every week. Plus doing regular visitation, leading Wednesday night Bible study and the men's breakfast on Saturday (where you are slated to talk about "purity"), picking the worship tunes, dropping by the MOPS coffee hour on Thursday, touching base with the work crew installing bushes around the sign out front, and writing that recommendation for the college senior looking to go to seminary.

Or let's say you awaken on Sunday morning hacking up a lung. If you are like most pastors, you are it, friend. Nobody gonna fill in for you. So you have to drag your Halls menthol drops, tissues, and feverish shivering body into the pulpit. And preach.

But wait, there's more. Maybe you just finished up a week of icy home life where your spouse and you are "working through" a myriad of relationship issues. You're talking politely to each other, but the tension is knife-able. And, lucky for you, this week's sermon in your nine-week series on the "Fruit of the Spirit" falls on—drat—kindness.

Meanwhile, we, your trusty congregation, just worked our own hard weeks, stayed out late on Saturday, woke up bleary-eyed, packed the recalcitrant kids into the car, and are now sitting in the pew smiling at you and waiting expectantly.

It is time for you to move us, challenge us, comfort us, and bring us to the throne of God. We want to be stimulated to think great thoughts. We want to meet God as a result of your words. We definitely want something fresh. Some of us need you to put it on the low shelf. But a lot of us have been around for a long time and need something profound or even complicated. Certainly, none of us wants anything clichéd. We each want you to meet our particular needs with this single sermon, even though we are a hundred different people.

And in three weeks, we have our congregational meeting to vote on your raise.

Eeesh. You've got one of the truly tough jobs. Yeah, Mike Rowe wouldn't want to try to be a preacher. He'd probably run back to milking yaks.

You Have to Bring Your A++ Game

If you are a preacher, you have my immediate admiration.

What you do matters. Really matters. That sermon time slot on Sunday has the potential to be the most important module in our week. Those of us sitting in the pews know that we should have daily quiet times. We know that we should listen to our Christian radio stations. We know that we should be in small groups or some kind of accountability relationship. But a lot of us aren't doing those things, at least not regularly.

But we do come to church on Sunday mornings to hear you preach.

Every profession has its "go-time"—that one activity or moment in which the practitioner has to bring his or her A++ game. For the product designer, it's that PowerPoint presentation to the senior vice president of product development. For the professor, it's that M/W/F 2:00 p.m. lecture. For the surgeon, it's that first scalpel slice through the patient's skin. For me, it's that moment I stand to address the jury at the start of a trial. For you, it's that twenty-six minutes on Sunday morning. You've got to bring your A++ game. Every time.

Whatever our profession, many of us spend our time sitting in meetings, making phone calls, researching online, reading job-related articles, e-mailing colleagues, drafting letters and other writing, taking out the trash, following or making plans, and interacting with fellow workers, customers, clients, bosses, end-users, competitors, the press, vendors, department chairs, technicians, support staff, and the postal carrier. In other words, no matter what most of us do, including pastoring a church, a lot of it is pretty normal, day-to-day, often mundane work. We should try to do it all well. The 80/20 principle allows us to do it decently, and that's usually plenty.

But that doesn't work for A++ time. It is my hope that this book will refortify you for that weekly A++ time in the pulpit.

The Big Idea of This Book

Everything you do with respect to your preaching should be the product of an *intentional* choice. The ironic thing is that even when you think you are not making choices intentionally, your actions reveal your intentions. Even if you don't mean them to. The essential principle upon which this book rests is the following: the key to good preaching is to make each of your decisions deliberately, consciously, intentionally, with the goal of communicating with the greatest effectiveness.

Do you move your hands while you preach? Why? Why not? Do your sermons have titles? Are they interesting? Why? Why not? Do you use illustrations? Why? Why not? Do you preach from a series of topics or from a book in the Bible? Why? Why not? Do you apply the sermon points to the lives of your congregation? Why? Why not?

Why do you do the things you do?

There is no "default" position on anything having to do with preaching. When it comes to preaching, you don't even wear default clothes. Think back to your last sermon. What were you wearing? Whatever it was, it was the result of a series of culturally driven, perhaps seeker-sensitive or emergent-church-prompted analysis. Ponder with me: Was what you wore attractional or missional? Perhaps your wardrobe choice was what your hearers expected you to wear and they would have been offended/distracted/upset if you wore something else. Whatever the case, there was a reason—conscious or unconscious—why you wore what you wore.

So then, why did you wear what you wore? Do you think that it made a difference? Why? Why not? Do you think anyone was helped by your choice? Are you sure one way or another? How are you so certain? The point is, you chose to wear what you wore. You chose that fancy or casual, tailored or off-the-rack, red or chartreuse, striped or polka-dotted, or paisley, silk, denim, or polyester piece of clothing.

Why did you wear that?

Why do you do the things you do?

Ask yourself two questions about everything you do with respect to your preaching: Is what I do the best way to communicate? And, is what I do hampering or helping my communication?

Back to your choice of clothing. Was it old? Was it worn? Was it creased? Have you worn it on many occasions? Was it flashy? Was it trendy? Was it conservative? Was it boring? What did it communicate? What did it tell your congregation about your preaching? What did it tell your congregation how you think about them? What did it tell your congregation how you think about the gospel?

Why do you do the things you do?

Hey Walters, That's Stupid

Okay, so you think that spending any time thinking about your clothes is stupid. Well then, you're going to hate this book. But before you put it on the re-shelve trolley, allow me a little story about John Wooden.

The late John Wooden is widely considered to be the greatest sports coach of all time. Even in his late nineties and long retired, he still commanded hushed tones of respect from lovers of the game of basketball and, frankly, most coaches from any sport. As the coach at UCLA, he had luminaries such as a young Lew Alcindor (later named Kareem Abdul Jabbar) and Bill Walton. His teams won the national championship ten times.

His players like to recount their first practice with Coach Wooden. He would have them sit down in bare feet with their shoes and socks next to them. He would then spend the next *half hour* teaching them how to put on a sock and a shoe. And when they were done with that, he'd move on to the left foot. No joke.

You might ask with well-meaning ignorance, why does it matter how an athlete puts on a sock, and what in the world about it could take so long to learn? But that's precisely the point. Wooden had noticed that basketball players were prone to blisters, and he concluded that it was often because their socks would be creased and folded in their shoes. Those blisters would hamper their performance or, worse, lead to graver injuries. Young college athletes had never been taught how to put on their socks and shoes properly—and in a way that would minimize injuries. He also observed that athletes often wore shoes one size too large. He addressed those impediments with each athlete he coached. Wooden's teams regularly won because they left nothing to chance. They exploited the advantage of every detail.

Why not approach preaching with the same single-minded focus? Why not analyze everything you do and choose to do it better and more effectively? Lord willing, you're going to spend the rest of your life preaching. Each improvement will multiply its benefit over that time. And your hearers will love you for it.

Hmm, Ever Wonder What They're Thinking?

I was at Walt Disney World a few years back, and one evening we dined at the Grand Floridian Café. As we ate, I noticed three clipboard-wielding Disney cast members standing discreetly behind a pillar. They spent about fifteen minutes observing us vacationers and taking notes on our dining behavior. They were gathering information about how we acted, what our needs were, and how well they were being met, all with the singular intention of improving our dining experience.

American companies spend billions of dollars on marketing research, employ the latest technologies for data mining on customer preferences, and solicit and analyze copious amounts of data to see if their products are attractive and useful to the ultimate consumer. One well-known social media site became worth over $500 billion because it, sometimes creepily, knows a half a trillion facts about you and me. Most companies welcome the information and the opportunity to make the kinds of adjustments and improvements that will keep their customers fulfilled and loyal.

In this book, for the price of a cheap date with your spouse, you have a one-man focus group. I'm just a guy in the pew. But I am passionate about preachers, preaching, and everything that comes with it. I think that what happens on Sunday morning when you get up in the pulpit is vital. And I believe that a little feedback from the pew may encourage you and help you do an even better job at the calling God has placed on your life.

I'm Just a Guy in the Pew, with a Twist

My love of preaching comes from being the son of a professor of homiletics. One of the pastors who read a draft of this book, and who had my father as his preaching professor, noted, "I had your dad for sixty hours of class time in preaching during my seminary days. You had him for twenty-nine years." That comment prompted me to estimate the number of hours I spent being trained homiletically by a man who spent forty years training preachers.

My education with him actually started before I was born. Literally. And a bit oddly. My father had read an article about a scientist who had begun his son's education *in utero* by lecturing him on physics through his mother's belly. So my dad started in on me with theology.

By the time I was five years old, he would spend at least an hour a day on "family devotions," which were essentially all-out sermon construction times. He would read the text, and my sister and I would strive to derive the main points and meaning from the Scriptures. He would then have us work out alliterative point headings. And these weren't one-word jobbers. He'd say, "There are four points in this text, each one 'The H_____ P_____ of the G_____.'" He was particularly pleased if we were able to come up with headings he hadn't considered. He would leave the house at 7:50 a.m. to go to his 8:00 a.m. preaching class, where he would challenge his groggy seminarians to try to best his kids' titles.

It will always be one of my abiding privileges that I was able to hear my father preach so many times. By the time I hit my late teens, I finally began to realize the uniqueness of the opportunity I was being provided, and I went to school on him.

My guess is that between those daily homiletic lessons, discussions about preaching, and then sitting under his preaching, I had well over ten thousand hours of homiletic training with Gwyn Walters, professor of preaching at Gordon-Conwell Theological Seminary. That's about 9,940 hours more than if I had just taken his seminary courses.

In addition, I've spent almost thirty years as a trial attorney and hundreds of hours in the classroom teaching law at a Christian liberal arts college. I've also coached preachers at their request and at the suggestion of their church leadership.

And, from time to time, I have been called up into the pulpit to preach.

As for the view from my pew: by this point, I've spent over half a century listening to preachers. I've heard some of the finest preaching this side of the Parousia. And, sometimes, the preaching is not so awe-inspiring. We pew-mates are the people for whom preachers spend countless hours of their lives preparing and then trying to reach, convince, persuade, cajole, encourage, and challenge. Sometimes they succeed; other times not so much.

I've sat in that folding chair, cushioned seat, theater-style flip down, outdoor rough-hewn wooden bench, grassy ground, and even once, the backseat of a Pontiac (at a Sunday morning drive-in service). I've seen preachers open the Bible to me in palpably powerful, life-changing ways.

I'm embarrassed to admit, however, that occasionally I've watched movies on the inside of my eyelids in an attempt to keep my brain operational pending the benediction. Given that I've never heard you preach, the following surely will not apply to you. I've occasionally wondered how I'd survived the periodic Sunday morning, amazed that thirty-four minutes of TV channel surfing at home on my leather sofa goes by like a cheetah on uppers; while with some thirty-four-minute sermons, time morphs into a glacial-speed, freeze-frame movie of a boy brushing his teeth. Important for dental hygiene, but just not that exciting.

On the other hand, I've been moved by preachers to see the grandeur of God, his immediacy in my life, his overwhelming love, his holiness, his desire for my good, my redemption, my sanctification, and my everything—all as a result of a pastor's exhilarating, careful, diligent, Spirit-filled, and stirring approach to the Sunday morning task of preaching the word in season and out of season.

It is my hope that as I share the view from my pew, you will also hear the myriad voices of your congregation, and you will gain much that will help you in your quest to preach ever more effectively. So that come Sunday morning, you will be able to lead us powerfully into the presence of God.

And all this from the privacy of your own home, while wearing your favorite sweatshirt.

A Few Suggested Guidelines in Reading This Book

My legal training tempts me to include a couple dozen disclaimers, explanations, and other limitations that serve only to drain the joy from any piece of writing. But I'm not getting paid by the hour here, so I'll toss in just a few.

The format of this book is simple. Each section focuses on one element of preaching or a single thought or concept. This book is decidedly not intended to be a comprehensive treatment of any of the points under consideration. Look to the left and right of this book on the "Preaching" shelf in the bookstore or webpage to find other, more exhaustive and erudite approaches.

Second, you will see that I write using the pronoun "you" often. I do that primarily because I'm writing to you. But if you think I am being unfairly or unduly negative, or if I am just plain annoying you, in those instances just imagine that I am writing to that preacher down the road at that church you have trouble liking. He's the real offender. Send him a complimentary copy of the book.

Third, I have deliberately made no attempt to clump the sections together by content. In fact, this book is meant to be read "on the fly." Read a section or two in the morning, and chew on it during the day. Although you may find some themes arising from the pages, each chapter is made to stand alone.

Fourth, I trust you will soon notice that I hold the Scriptures in the highest regard. If preachers are not preaching the Bible, then they are not preaching. Perhaps you will find it odd, therefore, that I do not cite more liberally from the Bible to make my points. If I have thought that the point I am making requires biblical support, then I have supplied it. But much of what is contained in the book is (a) irrefutable and therefore needs no textual support, or (b) completely a matter of taste and therefore incapable of proof-texting, or

(c) of a practical nature on which the Bible is silent. I'll let you decide which.

Fifth, since words are the preacher's tool, and sometimes the only tool that will work, I've made up a few for this book.

Finally, my prayer is simply that something, or perhaps even many things, between these covers will help you do the most challenging and fulfilling task imaginable—namely, bringing the word of truth to a world that so desperately hungers for it.

The Point of Preaching

What's the point of preaching? The question bears consideration for a number of reasons.

First, if you do not have a firm conviction of why you preach, then your preaching will lack power and focus and purpose. As dogs sense fear in a person, we congregants sense uncertainty and ambivalence in a preacher. If you are preaching on Sunday mornings only because that's what a pastor is supposed to do on Sunday mornings and for no other reason, then we, your hearers, will attend on Sunday mornings because that's what we are supposed to do. But we won't listen. At least not with any diligence or interest.

If, however, you know in the most global sense why it is that you preach to your beloved congregation every week, then that sense of purpose will permeate every aspect of your preaching, from your choice of text to your preparation of the sermon to your delivery.

Second, in a cultural milieu where news sound bites exceeding ninety seconds are considered "in-depth reporting" and song videos with camera pans longer than three to four seconds are seen as boring, it pays dividends to establish a sound apologetic when arguing the merits of standing in a stationary position and talking at someone for half an hour. The church is asking people to do something that virtually none of them ever does anymore: sit and listen to a near-motionless speaker for an extended period of time. With no interruptions. With no visual stimuli other than the upper half of a body. With no opportunity for questions or interaction. How wonderful for them if they can feel to their core why hearing your sermon can be one of the high points in their week.

Third, if you are not convinced of the point of preaching, then you will find it difficult to establish any metrics to know whether your preaching is doing anything helpful or valuable. Every Sunday morning sermon is like a coach's pregame speech. We are all on a team here. We've come to be inspired to achieve a common goal. To be reminded about why all the work is worthwhile. To be reminded about our various responsibilities. To be warned about hidden challenges. To be assured that past failures matter only insofar as they teach us. Above all, to meet with our Creator and hear from him, through your words. Having rehearsed those things, we will later be able to see whether we are achieving the goals set out for us.

You as a pastor will be able to know whether your preaching is doing what you intend it to do. Are people worshipping more vibrantly and intelligently? Are they experiencing the presence of God in their lives? Are they, by God's grace, becoming more Christlike? Are they reaching out with ever-increasing confidence and urgency to those around them and around the world who do not yet know Christ?

Once you have arrived at an answer as to why you preach, preach that point. There is no sense in keeping it a secret. Let us know from time to time why you climb into the pulpit each week.

To prime your pump on the point of preaching, I'll tell you what I long for each Sunday morning. I want to be ushered into the presence of our Creator and King. It should be an act of worship in itself and an invitation to worship together. Preaching should also open up God's word to me and give me consolation and conviction, help for my day-to-day trials, and preparation for my ultimate goal and reward: an eternity together with my Lord. Preaching ought to work to unify us as a congregation toward common goals, mutuality of living, and a drive to love. Finally, preaching should propel our worshipping community out into the waiting, needy world, equipped with the gospel and powered by the Holy Spirit and a God-given passionate love to reach the lost. I don't think I'm the only one who desires these things.

Will you succeed in leading us into all this each week? No. Will you succeed if those are not your goals? Probably. For as long as you are preaching out of the Bible, God will do his part. But your greatest loss will be the lost opportunity if you have not established firmly in your mind *why you preach.*

Preach from the Bible

Preach from the Bible. If you are not preaching from the Bible, then you are just preaching you. It may be that you and the Bible agree from time to time. But chances are that at some point, you and the Bible will disagree. At that moment, you are on your own. I might listen to you once or twice for entertainment's sake, but I'd be a fool to pattern my life after what you say.

I had a friend who preached a sermon once as a guest. Theologically, the congregation was not particularly liberal or particularly conservative. Nonetheless, as some of his hearers greeted him at the door at the end of the service, one of them exclaimed (in the presence of the senior pastor), "Wow! Nice sermon. It's great to hear a sermon from the Bible." Hard to imagine what people were hearing every week.

If you believe that the Bible is God's word and you accept from that essential belief those things that naturally follow—namely, that it is without error and that it is relevant—then what else could warrant your attention as the source of your weekly message?

The more we read the Bible, the more we are struck by its richness, its modernity (not in the philosophical sense, of course), its remarkable applicability to present circumstances, and its dumbfounding comprehensiveness.

Sit and watch a Dr. Phil talk show. Listen to the mess some poor couple or neighbors or family have made of their lives. If you are like me, you will try to anticipate what Dr. Phil is going to say. They've really made a mess out of that marriage, that friendship, that work environment, or that neighborhood. What kind of smart quip could I, like him, generate? What's the piece of advice that will unlock things for that person? Fifteen minutes into the show and I wonder what in the world I would tell these people. That Dr. Phil guy is sure super smart. Back from commercial break, he fires off advice, much of it good stuff. We wonder, how does he come up with that? The show succeeds in providing entertainment for two straightforward reasons. First, we all like a good train wreck. Nothing like a bit of schadenfreude to brighten our day. Second, however, we want to see Dr. Phil at work analyzing, probing, pushing, and then finally unlocking the mystery of why this particular motley bunch is so stinking dysfunctional and what they need to do about it.

Now, turn down the volume during one of those commercials and simply think in biblical categories. How does Scripture speak to this particular situation? What truths are applicable to sort out this specific mess? What stories from the Bible seem analogous to this one? What would Jesus say? What would Jesus do? As the answers start flowing, aren't you struck by how immediately germane those truths are? Doesn't it hit you that shifting your analysis to asking what the Bible says suddenly makes the situation a whole lot less complicated? It almost becomes child's play.

That is the beauty of the Bible that you bring to us each week.

That being said . . .

It's All Greek to Him

I have never been impressed by preachers who show me their underwear. For example,

> "The Greek word here is *philapiggery*. It appears seven times in the New Testament. Four of those times in Pauline Epistles. Sometimes it means hamburger and sometimes it means just plain ham. It is used once by John to refer to a meat byproduct, *spamkréas*."

Elegance happens when preachers clothe their expert exegesis in the English language, the language of their congregations. You are not lecturing. You are not presenting a paper. You are not vying for a post in the Classics Department of Harvard University. Instead, you are preaching. You are exhorting people from God's word so that their lives are changed and their hearts filled with grace and comfort.

We can agree that if you have not done the textual work, then your sermon soufflé will never rise. Thus we listeners are happy to assume that you know whether the word means "ham," "hamburger," or "meat byproduct." But the word study is not your outline. The exegesis is not your outline. Neither of those is your message. Rather, the message and then your sermon are constructed on the skeleton of diligent textual work.

Are there exceptions to this leave-the-Greek-at-home rule? Sure, if you are preaching to a group of Greeks. Or even if you are preaching to your Greek professor and a hundred of his Greek-teaching friends. And once in a great while, knowing the Greek word really can help make the point and get the message across.

I, and a good number of others who heard it, can still remember (which is perhaps the greatest compliment) a sermon my father preached in the 1960s at the historic Ruggles Street Baptist Church in Boston. He titled it "Paraclete or Parakeet," wherein he riffed on the difference between the originality of the Paraclete—the Holy Spirit—and his message, and a bird that speaks with no meaning and repeats only what it hears. Now that's not a bad use of the Greek.

A Perfect Illustration

Of course, there is no such thing. We all know that every illustration breaks down in the end. But try this one. I heard one preacher exhorting on the virtue of truth-telling and avoiding lies. Liars always seek the cover of darkness, he told us, because that's where they feel safe. Instead, he encouraged us, we should move to the light, where truth governs. And just when we needed one, he gave an illustration.

One of the results of having as much rain as we have had recently is that the grass grows really well. So yesterday I was out mowing my lawn. While I may not have as nice a lawn as many of you, it has been growing quite a bit. And as I was mowing, I saw a little toad. Since I didn't want to run over him, I gently coaxed him into the part of the lawn I had already cut. But the little toad kept jumping back into the deep dark grass, because that's where he thought he'd be safe. He didn't feel safe out in the short grass and the sun. But of course, the deep dark grass was where he was most in danger.

Let's analyze the illustration:

> "One of the results of having as much rain as we have had recently is that the grass grows really well."

He has appealed to a shared experience, the weather, and its effect on our gardens.

> "So yesterday I was out mowing my lawn."

Now he makes it personal and immediate. This is no illustration from a book or online illustration provider. No, this is the pastor's own life he is talking about. Hey, our pastor mows his own lawn. He's like us.

> "While I may not have as nice a lawn as many of you, it has been growing quite a bit."

Nothing wrong with a little self-deprecation.

> "And as I was mowing, I saw a little toad."

Introduces a character to what is now turning into a mini-drama.

> "Since I didn't want to run over him, I gently coaxed him into the part of the lawn I had already cut."

Note that we still don't know where he's going with this one, but we're completely in his hands, as was the toad.

> "But the little toad kept jumping back into the deep dark grass, because that's where he thought he'd be safe."

Zap. Eureka. Some in the congregation began to murmur as they saw the point illustrated.

> "He didn't feel safe out in the short grass and the sun. But of course, the deep dark grass was where he was most in danger."

The preacher made sure the point was conveyed clearly.

It is worth noting that there is no surfeit of information here. We aren't overloaded with what time of day it was, what kind of grass it was, whether it was in his backyard or side yard, or how many chores he had to do, or whether he'd been trying to mow the lawn for a week but hadn't had the opportunity. No, instead we are treated to an illustration with vivid detail and a little drama from a scene quite accessible to anyone who has walked on a freshly mowed lawn or seen a toad jumping around in deep grass. That, of course, essentially describes the whole congregation.

Make Sure It Is You Who Is Preaching

Who are *you*?

Your God-given "instrument" for preaching is you. That should excite you. God has given you all of your uniqueness in terms of experiences, abilities, family life, spouse, children, homes, stuff, education, jobs, body, looks, ancestry, ethnicity, race, and age. He has packaged it all uniquely, with nobody else exactly like you. All those influences have worked on you, producing you and only you. Even writing this gets me misty and makes me want to start singing, "It's a beautiful day in the neighborhood . . ."

But the point is a profound one for the preacher. Your calling in life, not just your job, is to hone all of that uniqueness, harness all of those attributes good and bad, and master them to preach God's word to whomever God puts in the pew in front of you next Sunday. No two preachers can ever preach exactly the same sermon. The congregation will hear both preachers differently, even if they preach from exactly the same manuscript. Just as no two instruments are identical in tone, timbre, sonority, pitch, and thus sound, so no two preachers can ever be identical.

In the end, be sure that it is *you* who is preaching.

My Start as a Sidekick

I don't remember how, when, or why it began. But one Sunday morning at the end of the service I, as a wee one, left my mother and sister in the pew and followed my father down the aisle as he strode out to the foyer. I stood by his side while he greeted each congregant as he or she filed out the door.

My father was a preacher who, during my life, preached twenty-one interims at different churches while they were between pastors. We would often accompany him to hear him. Though a Presbyterian himself, he happily took pulpits in nondenominational, Baptist, Congregational, and old-time gospel churches, or any other church that invited him.

Throughout his lifetime, many thousands heard him preach. But teaching was the ultimate leverage. Hundreds of thousands or more have sat under the ministry of pastors who first learned to preach at his feet.

My father had never asked me to stand by him. My mother never suggested it. My sister never tried it, even once. I just knew as a little kid that I wanted to be next to him, and I took that initiative one day after he'd preached. Tucked up next to him, I'd listen as the people thanked him for his morning's work and hear his humble replies: "Thank the Lord," "I hope it was of some help," or "Wonderful to see you; how is your husband doing?" And the best one: "This is my son, Meirwyn." If he needed anything, I would get it for him.

Looking back at it now, the weirdest part was not that I started doing it. It's that I never stopped. He died when I was twenty-nine, and whenever I was with him, I never missed a Sunday by his side.

First Words

Your first words matter.

Don't waste the tremendous opportunity that first words provide. Don't say what people are expecting. This is not an after-dinner speech where convention compels you to address the mayor, the chair, the trustees, the honored guests, members of the gardening club, and all pets present. This is the climax of the worship service. This is the preaching of God's word.

If you don't fashion your first words carefully, then you are giving up some serious real estate in the minds of your hearers.

I heard one pastor describe the first page of his sermon manuscript as a preamble, and he actually used the word *throwaway*. If it's a throwaway section to start your sermon, then why not do us all a favor and actually throw it away.

On the other hand, I know one guy who started a sermon at the memorial service for a seventy-six-year-old woman, saying, "There's a John Mayer song . . ." He then read the lyrics from a rock song that the deceased saint would never have heard during her life. But he knew that many of her children's friends knew the words. He took a stab that by starting first with quoting a quite secular rock artist, he might get the non-believing visitors to give him a chance.

For a sermon on Philippians 4:8–9, for example, start by holding up a large glass jar filled with hundreds of pennies and ask, "A penny for your thoughts? How much are your thoughts worth?" Then preach about thinking on noble, pure, holy, righteous, good things.

For a Super Bowl Sunday sermon, start off with the following, "At 6:23 p.m. tonight, Beyoncé will walk to the middle of an AstroTurf field and start singing the immortal words, 'Oh, say can you see . . . '" Don't worry, you'll find a way to segue into your topic.

The approach is relaxed for guest preaching. You may find that there is such a level of uncertainty or nervousness about who you are that you may need to shorten the distance, break the barrier. But even here, don't clichéd. We've all heard the preacher begin, "Well, it's a real privilege to be with you this morning. I'd like to thank my good friend Bob for the opportunity to preach . . . blah blah blah . . ." He's just joined the thousands of preachers before him in a pablumatic first-words cop-out. If it is really a privilege, then he should have painted that picture.

He could have tried this instead: "I remember being in a car with my dad when I was seven years old and driving by this church, and he turned to me and said, 'Poindexter, that's one of the great churches in the United States. The people love the Lord with all their heart.' So to be here now, forty-one years later, to preach our same Lord's words to you today is a tremendous privilege. My father and many of those saints have gone on to our Lord, but your faithfulness remains."

Which introductory remark catches us better? Which preacher do we want to listen to more?

Authenticity, for Real

I heard someone say that preachers can preach successfully only to someone within fifteen years of their age.

Don't believe it.

As I type these words, you are preparing a sermon for the Greatest Generation (a few), the Silent Generation, Baby Boomers, Generation X, Xennials, Generation Y/Millennials/Gen Next, iGen/Generation Z/the New Silent Generation, and Gen Alpha.

So many gens might drive one to gin. Or at least Excedrin.

The gospel, however, is applicable to everyone throughout all generations, regardless of time or place or any of the dozens of ways we characterize people. The trick is in fine-tuning your presentation to reach the truly unique characteristics of each generation. That's where the illustrations and applications do their heaviest work. As I discuss elsewhere, it is oddly true that by preaching to a specific person or group, you are more likely to reach everyone. Perhaps with regard to the challenge of being relevant to the different generations, we see that they are not separated by species but are all Homo sapiens who simply emphasize different things.

Millennials are known for needing to see authenticity in the preacher. That's perfectly fine because, although not overcome by that need, the Greatest Generation appreciates genuineness as well. My guess is that a Boomer is also happy with "keeping it real."

Millennials are accused of demonstrating certain narcissistic traits and being distinctively good at such vanity. If so, they may not be alone. I recall that in 1988, Bette Midler playing C. C. Bloom in the movie *Beaches* uttered the famous line, "But enough about me, let's talk about you . . . What do you think of me?" So perhaps Gen Y doesn't have the corner on self-absorption.

Don't be blind to the various distinctives of each generation, but relax and know that when you nail one, you nail us all.

"The Question"

During my college days, one of my professors became established as one of the foremost American historians alive. Twice a Pulitzer Prize-winning author, he had written seminal works on the American Revolution and was credited with significant advancements in historical methodology. His lectures were packed with knowledge and argument. And a bit of cynicism. By virtue of his achievements and force of personality, he had an ability to make grown men and women quake in his presence. Not to mention us poor collegians. We were happy just to take notes and run for the door at the end of the hour.

But his most intimidating moment came with his PhD students. These poor souls would have spent several years studying for their "generals," the exams that concluded their first level of graduate study, during which they had to become broadly expert in their field. After that, they would be given the opportunity to write their doctoral dissertation. Their greatest desire was to have this professor act as their advisor. During their time studying for the generals and for a bit thereafter, they would hone their thesis topic for their dissertation. What would be the question that they would study?

Keep in mind that they would end up spending the next three or four years of their lives and blood exploring their thesis topic. They would read every book, article, pamphlet, letter, and scrap of paper that could shed any light on their question. They would work late into the night. They would rise early to travel to dusty libraries the world over to hunt out crumbling papyri that would give them the unique angle, the one additional fact that would prove their argument.

This thesis was to be their crowning academic achievement. If they were among the fortunate few, their thesis would establish them as a world expert on the area of study. Their novel approach might even create a new historical methodology. Their thesis would become their first academic book. It would be their ultimate résumé in applying for the plum junior-level positions at the best universities in the world.

With so much hanging on their thesis, these students poured their all into framing their topic.

And when they were ready, each graduate student would finally appear before the professor to present the thesis question for his approval. The student would outline the argument. The professor would sit. The student would state the background. The professor would sit. The student, perspiring now, would explain how he or she would research the topic and what resources he or she expected to find and to use. The professor would sit. Silent.

And no matter how much they'd prepared, nothing could prepare them for what would come in the next moment; for finally, the professor would speak. And he, with lip curled satirically, would ask that most dismissive of phrases: "So what?"

So what! Who cares? What's the point? So what if you spend the next five years of your life studying for and writing this massive paper, what difference will it make? What will be your contribution to American history? Or moreover, the field of historical inquiry in general? Or most importantly, what will be your contribution to the world? Why bother with your insignificant pseudo-intellectual question?

Ouch.

If that clammy-palmed graduate student did not have a ready and persuasive answer for the question "So what?," it would be Groundhog Day as back he or she would go to spend another few sunless months drumming up a new thesis question.

Before you ever go up to a pulpit, you should have answered that question for your congregation. What do you want each hearer to receive from your preaching this coming Sunday? What do you think each hearer is supposed to do in response? What is your desired takeaway for each member of your congregation as they walk out your church doors? How will they be changed? If you haven't figured that one out, you don't have a sermon yet.

What's your message for this coming Sunday?

So what?

Preacher's Gotta Preach (Part 1)

My father once traveled to a remote, little church in the farmlands of Wales. He arrived outside the small stone chapel a quarter of an hour before the service was to begin. There was nobody there. Five minutes to service time. Nobody. With two minutes to go, here came a farmer. With nary a greeting, the old codger opened the chapel door and they both went in. The farmer nodded in the direction of the preacher's seat, and so my father took it.

Service time came and it was still only the two of them. So the farmer, sitting in the front pew, stood, turned around, and announced the first hymn. To the empty church. They both sang. The whole hymn. He sat down. My father read the Scripture. They both sang another hymn. Turning to the empty pews and with a clear voice, the farmer gave the announcements. To himself and to my father.

After all the preliminaries leading up to the sermon had been completed, my father offered to come down and do a Bible study with the two of them. No chance. The farmer sent him back up the stairs and demanded the full sermon.

So my father climbed back into the pulpit. And he preached.

What's the "Elephant in the Corner"? (Part 1)

It has always boggled my mind how I can attend church on a Sunday in the middle of the Olympics—a two-week extravaganza of extraordinary human achievement, toil, striving, success, and failure that comes around once every four years—and never hear one reference to the event in the sermon. Or perhaps there is a presidential election that week, or a natural disaster just killed thousands in Asia, or a precipitous financial downturn in the stock market has just ruined everyone's 401(k), and none earns an honorable mention from the pulpit.

What are we, those of us in the pews, thinking about this morning? Don't ignore it. Instead, use it as a way of reaching us.

If it is Super Bowl Sunday, then a good percentage of us are thinking about the game. You may have an evening service planned, but I guarantee that not all of us will be joining you. What a trove of illustrations you have available. What are the names of the teams competing? Any star players? Where is the game to be played? What are the human-interest stories circulating in the papers during the two-week drill up to the big day? What are we going to be cooking and eating tonight? Companies are paying millions of dollars for a thirty-second commercial, so surely you'll find something to say about that.

You can choose to tsk-tsk us silently, grumble about our lack of passion and commitment to church, and preach on while blithely ignoring one of the main events that excite us today. Or you can tap into that passion and channel it, leverage it, use it to grab our attention, and turn it toward God.

Even if it is not Super Bowl Sunday, you need to know what is going on today. What is the lead story on the 7:00 a.m. news? What's the headline in the Sunday paper? Did you have a big wedding of someone in your church yesterday? Did someone well loved in the congregation die last week? Was there a scandal that swept your region or the nation? Did some local guy or gal just "make good"?

How Many Points?

There is probably more ink spilled by preaching pundits on this question than any other, except perhaps alliteration (see below).

I sat through a seventeen-point sermon once. You may ask how I am certain that it was a seventeen-point sermon. A fair question, because arguably you might say that it came down to interpretation. Perhaps some items were sub-points, you might venture.

Ah, but in this particular sermon, the preacher made a point of counting. "For my next point, point number twelve, the writer of Philippians is saying . . ." I am not making this up. By the time the preacher announced number seventeen, I had been firmly convinced that no sermon ought to have seventeen points.

On the other end of the point spectrum is the idea of preaching one point, one idea. That, I can assure you, is far easier to swallow than seventeen points. If there is a single organizing principle or word or theme to the text, your congregation will be much more likely to remember it than seventeen such principles, words, or themes. You have forty-eight shots at these people every year. I imagine that you would be tickled to your pink cuticles if your parishioners remembered forty-eight things for every trip they take around the sun.

Personally, I like two, or preferably, three points. What's the big deal with three points?

First, people remember in threes.
Second, things come in threes.
Third, people remember in threes.

If your sermon does not have any points, then your sermon will, of course, be pointless.

Pee before You Preach, and Blow Your Nose

Can't put it more simply than that.

Honesty Honestly, Please!

Lake Wobegon is a marvelous community. Garrison Keillor's neighborhood is noteworthy in that "all the women are strong, all the men are good-looking, and all the children are above average." That phenomenon has been dubbed "the Lake Wobegon Effect."

In serving on a couple of pastoral search committees, I have had the opportunity to review the résumés and applications of scores of pastors. In my particular denomination, some applicants filled out a rather comprehensive survey in which they were requested to evaluate their particular gifts for ministry. For a list of ministry abilities they were asked to rate themselves on a scale of 1 (weak) to 7 (strong). There was quite a variation on many of the ministry initiatives. For example, the scores for youth ministry were all over the spectrum. But two things were for certain. Everybody rated themselves as a "1" for church administration. And for preaching, everybody rated themselves—wait for it—no worse than a "6," with most opting for a "7."

I listened to the tapes. Very few were "7s." In fairness to the candidates, they probably figured that no search committee would bother to listen to a "4" preacher. But I can assure you that if an applicant had said, "I used to be a '2' and now I'm a '4,' and I'm working on it," we would have listened with extra interest.

Give yourself a break and don't overestimate your ability in the pulpit. I suppose that if you do, you probably would not have read even this far. Be realistic, be open, be teachable until your last day of preaching, and put your confidence in God, not your abilities.

Plus, if by doing so you are able to move from a "4.2" to a "5.7," your ministry will be enhanced measurably and it will have been worth the vulnerability and humility.

Physical Preparation (Part 1)

The smell of bacon connoted "Sunday Morning" in our house. Harold J. Ockenga, then senior minister at historic Park Street Church in Boston, would be on the radio. My father would have been in his study reading his Bible and praying in anticipation of the morning's rigors of preaching. For a number of years, my job was to wake early to get the bacon on the stove. Sunday morning would find me peeling off those wonderful, greasy strips of salted heaven and laying them carefully in the hot frying pan. Soon the unmistakable, gorgeous aroma of sizzling, dead, cured pig filled the house. And my father would appear for his plate of Sunday-sermon supercharge.

Before the days of cholesterol, LDLs, and HDLs, my father always had eggs and bacon on Sunday mornings. He was a careful eater, always trim, and concerned for his body's health. But in those days, a "full breakfast" meant eggs, some kind of fried meat, toast, butter, jam, honey, and tea or coffee. He wouldn't think of venturing forth without full rations. Once he had that breakfast in the gut, he was ready for battle.

Then came all the articles on how bacon was evil, clogged arteries, and promised an early death. So my father switched to granola and fruit, including prunes. Oh well.

I think he eventually came to see that the squirrel food actually gave him more energy and concentration. And that was what mattered. I know he had enjoyed the eggs and bacon tremendously. But that was not the primary reason he ate it on Sundays. Rather, he ate what he thought would give him the best energy for the demands of the day. When technology and science pointed to a better alternative, he adopted it.

Physical preparation is key to ultimate effectiveness. Figure out what kind of breakfast gives you the most staying power throughout the morning. Then eat it.

Campbell's Chicken Soup and the Faint Evocation of a Metaphor

If you have ever had a can of Campbell's Chicken Soup, then you know you are having a very lucky day if you encounter a tiny piece of chicken from time to time. When I was growing up, there was a story going around that the Campbell Soup Company used only one chicken to make all of their chicken soup. They would just drag the same chicken through each vat of broth, leaving behind a distant hint of poultry. (They have since come out with a line of truly delicious Chunky Soups that serve only to buttress my point about the earlier versions.)

Some preachers take the same approach with their illustrations. Far from narrating the illustration from multiple facets and setting the scene with chunks of details, they simply mention the concept of the illustration and hope that this faint hint somehow clarifies their point.

One of the usual culprits of this phenomenon is an illustration that comes from a movie. For example, in talking about temptation, the preacher will say something like, "Satan often goes after our weakest points. Take the scene from *Star Wars* (*The Empire Strikes Back*) where Darth Vader tells Luke

Skywalker, 'I am your father. Come to the dark side.' Likewise, Satan goes after our vulnerabilities."

Phew. Way to paint a picture. If George Lucas felt he needed two *movies* to get to that punchline, then what makes the preacher think that he can do it in two *short sentences*? The illustration is marginally helpful if you have seen the movie. Nearly useless if you have not.

Instead, spend time describing the facts that make the illustration more than just a passing mention. Picture the scene in your mind as you describe it. Forget about the words on your manuscript. What do you see in your brain? Let us in on the secret. What does Darth Vader look like? What is he doing? Where is Luke Skywalker? During this conversation, is he sitting on a beach chair reading a romance novel, or is he hanging on a pole by his one remaining arm over a seemingly bottomless pit? Does that matter? Of course it does. Pick out the facts that are important, the ones that drive the story, that build the dramatic tension. Flesh it out, my friend, flesh it out. Your point in using the *Star Wars* story is to engage us in understanding that Satan often chooses our most vulnerable moments to attack. How can we feel our own helplessness if we have not felt Luke Skywalker's first?

Hands Up (Part 1)

History has been made and punctuated with a gesture of the hand.

God sparking life into Adam on Michelangelo's grand Sistine Chapel painting.

Two black champion athletes standing on the podium in Mexico City at the 1968 Olympics and igniting wide-ranging emotions, controversy, and introspection when, during the medal ceremony, they each bowed their heads and silently raised a single, black-gloved fist to the sky.

Mr. Spock's Vulcan salutation.

President Nixon in historic irony waggling two fingers in a "victory" sign as he boarded a plane after his humiliation and resignation from the most powerful position in the world.

Argentinean soccer legend Maradona's hand-"header" scoring, or what became known as the "Hand of God" goal in the 1986 World Cup.

A tiny hand of hope belonging to a baby reaching through the incision in his mother's belly and clasping the surgeon's finger, establishing one of the most powerful and iconic arguments in the abortion debate.

Hands speak. What are your hands telling us?

Live and Breathe It before You Preach It

It is easy to see when preachers have gnawed at the bone of the text and really spent time applying it to their own lives. There is a more profound passion and delight in the preaching. There is an evident personal appreciation of the importance of the text. There is the heightened sense that these preachers "get it."

The reasonable objection may be, "But how can I live every single text I preach? I'm just one person." The answer is found in the fact that every text is immediately applicable, whether in response to present life circumstances or sequestered as a storehouse treasure to be called upon in future situations. Meditate on the text you are going to preach. Read it on Monday morning as part of your devotions. Chat about it with your spouse, your family, or a good friend. Mull it over in your mind on Tuesday. Even when your sermon is done by Saturday, continue to think about the text.

God encourages us to meditate on his word. We can know that there are deep spiritual blessings that will result. Show us that you know that to be true out of personal experience.

The Good and Otherwise of the "Derby Sermon"

In England, the Derby is the premier horse race. Your "Derby Horse," if you are so fortunate to own one, is a great horse with a chance to win. In Britain over the past century, far more than here in the United States, many chapels did not have a full-time minister and instead filled the pulpit with a succession of itinerant preachers. As they traveled from church to church filling empty pulpits, these preachers would sometimes develop the reputation of having a "Derby Sermon"—the one sermon they would trot out when they needed to impress the congregation.

Over here in the US, the Derby Sermon worked pretty well for men such as Russell Conwell and his "Acres of Diamonds." Conwell is said to have preached what became one of the most famous sermons in history over five thousand times between 1900 and 1925. I imagine by just the hundredth time, he had gotten the pacing, phrasing, and emphasis down cold.

There is nothing wrong with having a sermon more or less ready to go in the event that you are called on short notice to cover for a sick pastor. Being prepared in season and out of season means you can stand at a minute's notice to bring a message of encouragement to the brothers and sisters assembled before you.

I knew a biblical scholar with few peers, and his insights into Scripture established new paradigms for biblical interpretation. A devout and humble man, he unlocked the Bible for generations. But he also had a rather amusing system when it came to preaching. I don't think he would have described himself as a preacher, but his position allowed him that opportunity once in a while at various churches near his home. He did not have an extensive stable of sermons, and none of them was a Derby Sermon, so he kept a chart on the wall of his study detailing which sermon he had preached in which church. When he was called to fill one of those pulpits, he would consult his chart and pull out of his files one of the sermons he had not yet preached there. That way he could avoid unwittingly preaching the same thing twice.

Just don't forget that on the day of the race, even the Derby Horse must be prepared for the particular conditions of the day, the state of the track surface, the temperature, the weather, the position at the gate, and so on. Even Conwell knew to interject the name of the city where he was preaching. Make sure your Derby Sermon has a few blank slots for congregation-specific allusions. Then preach the eternal truths with confidence.

Application = Afterthought

We come on Sunday mornings to be changed. So it is one of the more perplexing realities that many preachers often do not spend quality time on their applications. Some simply don't get around to it. And there are members of a truly curious subset who go all the way and assert that they do not think it is their role to apply the sermon. I've run into a few preachers who state with a certain dismissive "spirituality" that their job is simply to explain the Scriptures and then to "allow the Holy Spirit to apply it to each hearer's life."

The reality is, however, that this small band of preachers doesn't truly believe they are freed from the obligation of application "because it is God's job." I think they are really just camouflaging a fear of inadequacy. It's one challenge to figure out what the text means. It's yet another challenge to find illustrations to convey that meaning. But it can be a head-scratcher to figure out how each of the hearers will actually get some mileage out of the sermon. "I've got 328 parishioners on a Sunday morning. How can I possibly figure out what they each need to do to actually change their lives? I'd have to be a psychic." These preachers are the Little Trains That Couldn't. "I know I can't, I know I can't . . . See, I couldn't."

The argument also hides a fear of one's congregation. "If I actually made these applications week in, week out, I'd end up stepping on a few toes." If preachers keep their sermons general, then they generally won't encounter too many irked or even irate hearers. And, generally, the congregation will, in general, not grow (generally speaking).

But there is a cost that comes with such fear. It's less likely that the pastor will receive comments at the foyer door like: "Pastor, it was as if you prepared that sermon just for me." Or, "As a result of today's sermon, I'm going to invite those neighbors over for coffee," or "talk to that coworker about the Lord," or "call my sister who I haven't talked with in fourteen years to apologize," or "not go into the office on Saturday and instead take my teenage boy camping," or "increase my giving to the church in the increments you set out."

Further, the anti-application perspective is not logical. Since the Holy Spirit is capable of anything, why not just read the biblical text in Greek to the congregation and then sit down. If God can (and he does) apply his truths, then surely he can (and will) exegete. I bet if we wait long enough, he'll illustrate the sermon as well. Taken to its logical extreme, we could just let God pick the text and then preach the whole kit and caboodle by himself. Each Sunday sermon would then be a preacher's version of John Cage's groundbreaking solo piano piece, *4'33"*. Go ahead, stand up in the pulpit, say nothing for twenty-two minutes and then sit down. God will fill in the rest.

To apply well requires spending valuable time and energy getting to know the people who sit in the pews from week to week, understanding their specific challenges, and staying sensitive to those challenges as each person matures or just plain gets older. Sins sometimes seem like viruses: once we've defeated one, it mutates into another version, at some times slightly and other times more radically. The application of God's truth to each of these new mutations requires a freshness and creativity that is flat out work. Some preachers are not willing to go that far.

But you, I'm sure, are made of sterner mettle than that.

Hands Up (Part 2)

When watching some preachers, I sometimes feel like a policeman shouting: "Put your hands up where I can see them!" Perhaps it is simpler for those who are Welsh or Italian or Middle Eastern, where half of all communication is done with hands. But whatever your cultural background, your hands are your most able interpreter and you should use them to your advantage.

Put the book down and examine your hands. How big are they? Are your fingers long or short? Are your hands damaged in any way? Are they flexible or stiff? Do you like your hands?

Are you pleased with how you've used them in the past? Is God pleased with your hands? Ask him now to rededicate them to his uses and to communicating his gospel.

Now go find a mirror and start playing with your hands. Let's make them go all loquacious on us.

Variety is the spice of gestures. We've all seen the politicians who apparently get some kind of paralysis from the wrist to their fingertips. They use exactly the same hand motions whether they are expounding on wheat subsidies, dedicating a new playground, or proposing bombing evil dictators. Don't fall into the same gesticulatory rut.

Straighten your elbows.

Bend your fingers.

Open your hands. Keep your fingers together. Now spread them apart. Keep your ring finger and pinkie together and your thumb, index, and middle fingers together and say "Na-Nu Na-Nu" to greet other Orkans in the room.

Close your hands.

Clasp both of your hands together. Flatly.

Or with interlocking fingers. Or with only fingertips touching.

Use your left hand.

Use your right hand.

Face your palm up. Face your palm down.

Put your right hand in, put your right hand out, put your right hand in, and shake it all about. Do the hokey pokey . . . That's what preaching's all about.

Just kidding about that last bit. But give those hands a workout. Experiment now with the effect of different motions. How do you feel? What are you saying? Are you using your hands differently now from how you usually do in the pulpit. Why? Why not?

The Pulpit Isn't for an Oscar

There is a critical difference between eloquence and acting. The same is true for emotion versus emoting. Never cross the line or you will lose our respect. Do not let your lip waver unless you are caught by that emotion. Do *not* act angry; instead, make sure your conscience is truly stirred. Then *be* angry.

There is a fraudulence to acting in the pulpit. By this I do not mean, of course, that you cannot playact for a moment for the purpose of bringing life to the text or to your point. But when it is you speaking, make sure you are speaking what you genuinely believe and in a manner consonant with your belief.

There is nothing more authentic than the gospel. There is nothing more real than the work of the Holy Spirit in the lives of God's creatures. There is nothing more sincere than God's words to us. You will give lie to all that if you act.

Pray that God will give you freedom to feel intensely the truths you are presenting and that those feelings will be visited in your expressions, your body language, your tone, and even your language.

Hosea wept as he preached. Isaiah was fearful. Paul at times was urgent, even strident in his tone and delivery. Jeremiah covered the vast array of emotions. Do you think he preached the message "Attack the land of Merathaim and those who live in Pedok. Pursue, kill and completely destroy them" (Jer. 50:21), while placidly dangling a toothpick in his mouth? Of course he didn't, and neither should you. On the other hand, do you think that David recited or sang "The Lord is my shepherd, I shall not want" (Ps 23:1), while grimacing fiercely and punching the air with karate chops? Doubtful.

Authenticity demands preaching with the appropriate emotion just as much as it prohibits acting.

Don't act. Be real.

Illustrations: Where in the World Can You Find One?

Finding illustrations is as much science as it is art. Although some preachers are just plain gifted at seeing illustrations, I firmly believe that all preachers called by God to the pulpit will be able to illustrate their message. It just takes a few principles and some practice.

First, practicing (right) makes perfect, or at least interesting. When you read a magazine, look at an advertisement and create three illustrations from it. How would you include today's newspaper headline into your sermon? Walking through the mall, what are you seeing and experiencing that could produce an illustration? How could you use what that kid just said to her mom? Look up from this book right now and make up an illustration for "futility" from something in your environment. Do the same for "success."

Second, *anything* is fodder for illustration. That billboard on the way to church. A TV commercial. Your child's soggy baseball glove on the driveway. An advertising slogan or a campaign. A brand-new cookbook. A brand-new cookbook compared to your old Julia Child cookbook handed down by your mother. A brand-new online cookbook on a cooking website compared to a brand-new Barnes and Noble bought cookbook compared to your old tattered, batter-spattered Julia Child cookbook handed down by your mother. That old dog sitting on your neighbor's porch. The new dog that just pooped on your front lawn . . . again. That phone call from a high school classmate you haven't seen in years. A pile of old magazines. The fact that you have a pile of old magazines. The type of magazines. A Hummer. A Hummer 2. A Hummer 3. The smell of home fries wafting from the diner down the street. The lunar eclipse last night. The crisp feel of a new $20 bill versus a worn sixty-seven-year-old dime. The rusting '55 Chevy truck in the field half a mile from the church.

Own them for your sermon.

What would that phone call from your classmate illustrate? What about it will help you convey a point?

- Is it that you had not heard from that friend for twenty-four years?
- Was she an old girlfriend? And what did your wife say when the call came in?
- Did that classmate bear news that shocked or surprised?
- Did the call bring to mind great memories? Did it uncover forgotten hurts?
- Was there reconciliation of an old dispute?
- Was the intention of the call simply to find out details about an upcoming reunion, but it ended up triggering a whole range of unexpected emotions and expectations?
- Were you surprised at how unmoved you were?

Now advance to the point you are making: The sweetness of reunion and an eye to heaven's reunion. The balm of righting past wrongs and the benefit of persuading others to do so. The fact that while we have breath it's never "too late." That God calls us to a ministry of reconciliation. The call to be people of encouragement. The beauty of trust between spouses. The need to feel life.

Or what different points can we illustrate out of that old Chevy?

- It evokes a simpler time and provides us with memories of drive-in theaters, soda jerks, buzz cuts, and more.
- It tells us that someone can't let go of something.
- To some of us, it is an eyesore; to someone else with the talents and abilities, it represents a prize-winning entry at a car restoration competition.
- Perhaps it embodies the hope of regeneration.
- On the other hand, maybe looks are deceiving and it only appears like it needs a ton of work; and perhaps with only a quart of oil, a new battery, and some tires it would be good to go.
- The differences between that truck and a brand-spanking new version; simplicity versus complexity; is new always better?
- The rust has destroyed what was once someone's proudest possession.
- You tell me. What do you see in that old Chevy?

If you feel that you do not have a readily homiletic mind, then this kind of exercise will develop your homiletic muscles.

Everything is fodder for an illustration.

Third, don't collect illustrations. By these I mean tried-and-true illustrations that have withstood the test of time and been used in sermons from Alaska to Zimbabwe. I guarantee that if you bought this book off the bookstore shelf, then within three feet of this tiny tome were a half dozen books of nothing but illustrations. How about the "footprints in the sand" one, "the pilot of the plane" one, the "Niagara tightrope walker" one, or the "can't take gold bricks to heaven" one? We've all heard them, or at least variations of them. These stock illustrations significantly reduce any impact, compared to one you produce especially for this congregation with this sermon. There's also something slightly plagiaristic about the whole thing.

Having said all that, I'll probably write a book of illustrations one of these days and urge you to buy it, on the theory that some kind of illustration is better than no illustration at all. But I'll also urge you to rework them to fit your specific point and make them as fresh as possible.

Usually, the first illustration that comes to mind stinks. It is probably trite, clichéd, overused, and boring. Yawn. Go deeper.

Take your illustrations from your life. Pardon the obvious, but doing so will personalize the sermon. There is an intimacy and an immediacy to letting the congregation in on your life and your experiences when you seek to translate scriptural truths into usable chunks.

Fourth, *do* collect illustrations. By that, I mean fresh new ones. In the course of living, as you run into funny situations, see curious signs, experience something new, hear a unique story, notice changes in the world around—in short, as you live life—preserve those vignettes for use down the road. All these things could make for good illustrations for some future sermon. Jot them down, cut them out of the newspaper, print them from the website, and then file them. It's that last task that will be challenging. Perhaps you are database savvy enough to catalogue them in your computer under a host of different possible subject headings or keywords. Maybe you are a whizbang with manila folders. The key will be retrievability. Will you be able to find that illustration later? Even if you don't end up using them, however, the exercise of collection and categorization can only enhance your awareness of illustrations in your daily life.

If "Meeting Jesus" Is All We Need, Then Why Did Jesus Spend So Much Time Applying His Truths?

What does the Bible say about applications?

First, we are to "speak the truth in love." Explicit in the context of the passage and implicit in that command from the letter to the church at Ephesus is the fact that we as believers will from time to time see our fellow brothers and sisters failing to walk according to their inheritance. Paul compares the Ephesian Christians to Gentiles who are darkened in their understanding, engaging in all manner of impurity and giving themselves over to sensuality. We, on the other hand, are expected to "put off" our old self and "put on the new self." Paul exhorts Christians to make changes to their lives to bring them into congruity with God's expectations.

What does that look like? How can that be applied to our lives? Read on after Ephesians 4:15 and you will see Paul applying the exhortation. For starters, we will stop sinning in our anger. We will speak truthfully to our neighbor, a fellow member of one body. We will not let the sun go down while we are still angry. We will not let the devil get a foothold. If we have been stealing, we'll steal no more. We will do something useful with our hands. We will make sure that we have something to share with those in need. Knowing what we know about Paul, we can safely assume that he was priority-mailing each of those applications to a specific person or two in his audience churches.

So we see that "speaking the truth in love" for Paul includes exhorting specific changes and actions from each believer. My guess is that if Paul preached long enough for Eutychus to go to sleep, then he was probably getting pretty specific on applying God's truths to the lives of his hearer!

Mindless repetition of theological truisms without telling us what to do with them is not preaching.

Look as well at the example of our Lord. The parable of the sower gives us some insight into how Jesus preached. Jesus tells the crowd about a farmer who goes out to sow his seed, with some falling on the path to be trampled or eaten by birds, some on the rock where they initially spring up but then wither, some among thorns where they first grow but then are choked by the weeds, and finally some on good soil where they yield a hundred times bounty.

Then Jesus turns to his disciples and continues his sermon. He assures them that knowledge of the secrets of God's kingdom have been given to them. Then, assuming that this parable is more than simply a description of spiritual reality, he shows how the truths apply to his hearers. His elaboration of the illustration lays out in detail the seed's environment in the life of the hearer and how the path, rock, thorns, and good soil will be evident. How does this parable apply to the hearer? Don't let the devil snatch away the truth. Don't get all excited about the truth but then run away at the first sign of trouble. Don't allow life's worries or, conversely, life's treasures and pleasures to choke out the truth in your life. Instead, live with a noble and good heart, hear the truth, retain it and persevere, and by doing so see the truth produce a bountiful crop in your life.

We know that we have only a very small portion of Christ's words committed to print. John tells us that if all that Christ did were written down there would not be room in the whole world for the books. We can surmise that Jesus spent a great deal of time further applying his truths, delving into the details of his hearers' lives, and showing his listeners how each particular truth applied to their lives.

At the end of the day, it is impossible to explain the Scriptures without applying them.

What's the "Elephant in the Corner"? (Part 2)

August 31, 1997, was a Sunday, and I awoke particularly early that morning in Milwaukee, Wisconsin. I had been invited to preach to the annual gathering of Welsh-Americans at the Welsh National Gymanfa Ganu bilingual church service, probably mostly as a fit of nostalgia. My father had been a beloved "pastor" to this once-a-year gathering, having preached numerous times over the preceding twenty-five years, and this morning marked the fourth anniversary of his passing into glory. This was the first time I would preach to this gathering and, frankly, I was feeling some performance anxiety (see elsewhere on that sin).

There would be as many as one thousand who would pull themselves out of bed in time to attend. Many would be primarily interested in the Welshness of the event rather than the gospel. The attendees ranged from actual Welsh men and women who were newly arrived "off-the-boat" subjects of the Crown and feeling homesick for anything Welsh, to fourth- and fifth-generation farmers from Iowa trying to maintain some connection, however tenuous, to their Welsh heritage. The weekend was filled with seminars on Welsh things old and new, banquets, "celebrities" from Wales, British accents, and general Welsh merriment.

The Sunday morning service gave the attendees an opportunity to hear some "Welsh preaching" and reconnect to a time when the church mattered in Wales. Although we should try to create every sermon with care and diligence, there are times and settings where any of us goes a bit overboard. And this was one of those times for me. Obsessing would only begin to describe it. I had prepared the sermon meticulously.

I was also particularly diligent, because I had to meet the challenge of interweaving the Welsh and English languages while preaching the sermon. In a real way, I had to preach two sermons simultaneously, with one complete sermon for those who only spoke English, and a "second," simultaneous sermon that avoided mere repetition or translation for those who spoke both languages. Having been given a year's warning, suffice it to say that by 5:30 a.m. on August 31, 1997, the sermon was absolutely "in the can."

My title was "A Feast for the Ayes/Hwyl y'r Gwyl," taken from Matthew 22:1–14, the remarkable parable where the father invites many distinguished guests to his son's wedding banquet. All of them decline for what appear to be ridiculous reasons, and some even kill the servants carrying the invitations. In response, and only after killing the worst of the bunch, he sends out his servants to invite anyone else they can find. Successful at their task, the servants pack the hall with all sorts of guests. The host then turns his attention to one man who is not properly dressed for the occasion and after querying how he was admitted "without wedding clothes," he orders the man bound and thrown where there will be weeping and gnashing of teeth.

It may be difficult for you to appreciate the Welsh and their love, some say madness, for language. But I knew that for this particular sermon this cultural reality allowed me a rather unique setting to go a bit crazy with my sermon point titles. I deal with those elsewhere in this book, but this digression is helpful to address my main point here of not avoiding the elephant in the room. My English point headings were as follows:

- An Invite
- Acts of Spite
- Shows of Might
- Those Out-of-Sight
- Dress That's Right
- Endless Delight

The Welsh headings were similarly alliterative.

Being a bit nervous, I rose from bed especially early in order to take a walk through the then empty downtown area, breathe the fresh morning air, and pray about the service and exertions to come. I walked along the sidewalks, looking for a park or city garden to introduce a bit of green to the time. It was a beautiful morning with the sun rising, the air clear, and the sky transitioning to a translucent blue. Aside from the occasional delivery or dump truck in the distance, it was a quiet urban start to a Sunday.

As I came to a corner, I spotted a cluster of newspaper boxes. Always curious to know what is going on in the local area, I walked over to read the day's headlines. The city's Sunday newspaper with its front page pressed against the inside of the glass screamed out at me: *PRINCESS DIANA DEAD*.

The headline stunned me. Say what you might about not caring about the monarchy, criticize Princess Diana's lifestyle, pooh-pooh celebrity-ism all you wish, but the fact remains that this was one of those events so riveting—like the Challenger explosion or JFK's assassination—that people remember where they were when they heard the news.

Now also keep in mind that but for the most nationalistic Welshman, Diana was the *Princess of Wales*, and I was about to preach to a thousand people of Welsh extraction. And every single one of them would be processing this staggering news.

But my sermon was all done, zipped up, tight as a drum, timed exactly, practiced endlessly and therefore unalterable. Well of course that latter bit is not true, because that wouldn't be preaching, now would it? So, standing there on the cracked concrete sidewalk staring at the newspaper box, I spent some time choosing a few options of where I could incorporate this tragic reality.

Once the service began, I caught a break when, prior to the sermon, the gentleman convening the service made mention of Princess Diana's heartrending death and even, I think, held a moment of silence. The elephant had been acknowledged.

So I could wait until I came to the point of "Dress That's Right" for the banquet. I gently developed how we were all mourning the death of a woman of unparalleled class and someone who was known for always being beautifully dressed for whatever occasion awaited. And then I went right at the gospel by describing the only type of dress that mattered for her now was the robe of righteousness that Christ has prepared, and was she dressed right? I took care not to hint at or offer an answer.

At that moment, if they hadn't done so yet, the hearers went from being mere observers to being participants. They were forced to channel their grief and shock into what they were hearing. The gospel mattered for them in real and concrete terms. This parable connected to their actual life experiences, a terrible one only a few hours old.

The elephant had led us directly to the gospel's challenge to life and death.

If you need more convincing, go to the greatest preacher to have lived. Jesus knew to address those kinds of events. He preached about a tower that fell and killed "innocent" people and in doing so went to the heart of the confusion such an event triggered. He addressed directly what was happening in Jerusalem even as he walked into the city to meet his death. He engaged political and religious leaders often at the gut of their opposition. He stopped a discourse to yank a short guy out of a tree. He pulled his examples from within arm's reach. He was forever willing and able to draw upon his immediate environment for entre into the gospel.

Whatever you do, don't avoid the elephant. Make his big gray presence in the back pew work for you, not against you.

Silence (Part 1)

Sometimes the most powerful thing you can say is nothing.

Silence (Part 2)

Let me violate that rule and elaborate.

We humans feel that we must keep our lips moving and our voices generating sound waves, or something unmentionably dreadful will happen. Perhaps people will stand up and leave. Perhaps if we stop speaking, we'll never be able to get started again.

But silence is to speech what white, the absence of color, is to painting. It is the light of speech.

Silence gives rest. It allows the hearer to reflect for a second longer on what has just been said.

Knowing when to inject silence is part art.

Certainly, as you enter areas of particularly heightened emotions, pauses can expand the congregation's experience of the emotion. Are you seeking joy? Fear? Comfort? Give them time to engage those emotions and feel them. Speak too soon, and the moment is lost forever.

Titles Matter

Just look at all these little bits and bobs of advice. If you are jumping around and not reading every single one in order, you've probably chosen to read some of these chapters solely based on the title. And you've probably skipped a few because the title didn't trigger any curiosity. While an exciting title will not guarantee an interesting sermon, a snoozer title almost always presages a boring preacher.

A sermon on Jesus walking on water? "The Imperfect Storm."

A sermon on the heavenly host announcing Christ's birth to a crew of shepherds? "The Angel Angle."

Are these great titles? I don't know. But they sure beat "Lord Over Nature," "Angels and Shepherds," or other riveting headings, such as "Thou Shalt Not Lie" or "No Condemnation."

Don't forget that you are preaching to a generation of multitechers for whom overstimulation is a byword. Can they possibly get excited for a sermon titled "Grace Abounds"? You can be mad at your hearers for being trite and trivial, lacking in profundity and more interested in their makeup than making up with the Lord of the Universe. Or you can realize that we are all a bit like that ourselves and help us escape our ennui.

Probably within fifteen miles of you is a church with one of those outdoor glass-encased bulletin boards showing the name of the church, the names of the pastor and organist and the times for Sunday school and services and one other thing—the coming week's sermon title. And unlike the forty-two other glass-encased bulletin boards that you see on the way to and past this particular church and that you never look at, this one is always pun-ny or arresting or quizzical or funny. Perhaps in the privacy of your car you may criticize the church each time you pass the church: "They're so rigid and fundamentalist they probably starch their boxers," or "They're so liberal, that's a social club, not a church." If you are like me, however, you always read the sign and chuckle. And secretly, you wonder what the sermon is going to be like.

Church signs found on the Internet:

- "ATM Inside. Atonement, Truth, and Mercy."
- "Snowmobiles Thrill? I like Stormy Sea Walking: Jesus."
- "Prayer: Wireless Access to God with No Roaming Fee."

Did you chuckle more about those than your congregation did for your last week's sermon title?

Preacher's Gotta Preach (Part 2)

Sharks die if they don't keep swimming. (That's actually a myth, but it works for my point here.) Preachers go all raisiny if they can't preach.

My father probably lacked having a pulpit to preach in only ten Sundays in his fifty-four-year preaching ministry. Yes, he did preach on his three-day weekend-straddling honeymoon and also a few weeks later on the *HMS Queen Mary*, at the captain's invitation, during his first transatlantic voyage with my mother to the United States. He preached on any family birthday that had the misfortune of falling on a Sunday. He also preached when we traveled, since the preaching was usually the reason for the traveling.

And although an otherwise calm, gentle, and patient man, if he didn't get a chance to preach on a Sunday morning, he would get, shall we say, grumpy.

Reading Scripture

Many pastors overlook the advantage to reading Scripture well. Far from seeing it as the "opening argument" for their entire sermon, or their first shot at tilling the brain soil of their hearers for the truths that are about to be planted there, they seem to view it as a laborious but necessary part of their Sunday morning duties. They either rush or plod through their text without much expectation of what they are accomplishing. Seldom do we eagerly anticipate their readings. Seldom do they leave us with a sense that they have just read some words that this very morning are going to give us hope, vivify our beings, prick our consciences, feed our souls, and change our lives.

We could make a good deal of the fact that Scripture, being God's very words to us, deserves to be read well and indeed demands as much. When you read well, you communicate your love, affection, respect, and awe of the word. That principle should be obvious and should be enough to provoke extra attention to the task.

But an equally primary concern here is that an excellent reading of the Scripture, particularly the Scripture upon which you will preach, sets up your entire sermon.

So, how should you read?

As an example, let us take the account of Elijah immediately after his victorious demonstration of God's power to Jezebel's prophets on Mount Carmel. Read the following passage from 1 Kings 19:1–18 aloud in a monotone voice:

> [1]Now Ahab told Jezebel everything Elijah had done and how he had killed all the prophets with the sword. [2]So Jezebel sent a messenger to Elijah to say, "May the gods deal with me, be it ever so severely, if by this time tomorrow I do not make your life like that of one of them."
>
> [3]Elijah was afraid and ran for his life. When he came to Beersheba in Judah, he left his servant there, [4]while he himself went a day's journey into the desert. He came to a broom tree, sat down under it and prayed that he might die. "I have had enough, LORD," he said. "Take my life; I am no better than my ancestors." [5]Then he lay down under the tree and fell asleep. All at once an angel touched him and said, "Get up and eat." [6]He looked around, and there

by his head was a cake of bread baked over hot coals, and a jar of water. He ate and drank and then lay down again.

7The angel of the LORD came back a second time and touched him and said, "Get up and eat, for the journey is too much for you." 8So he got up and ate and drank. Strengthened by that food, he traveled forty days and forty nights until he reached Horeb, the mountain of God. 9There he went into a cave and spent the night.

And the word of the LORD came to him: "What are you doing here, Elijah?"

10He replied, "I have been very zealous for the LORD God Almighty. The Israelites have rejected your covenant, broken down your altars, and put your prophets to death with the sword. I am the only one left, and now they are trying to kill me too."

11The LORD said, "Go out and stand on the mountain in the presence of the LORD, for the LORD is about to pass by." Then a great and powerful wind tore the mountains apart and shattered the rocks before the LORD, but the Lord was not in the wind. After the wind there was an earthquake, but the LORD was not in the earthquake. 12After the earthquake came a fire, but the LORD was not in the fire. And after the fire came a gentle whisper. 13When Elijah heard it, he pulled his cloak over his face and went out and stood at the mouth of the cave. Then a voice said to him, "What are you doing here, Elijah?"

14He replied, "I have been very zealous for the LORD God Almighty. The Israelites have rejected your covenant, broken down your altars, and put your prophets to death with the sword. I am the only one left, and now they are trying to kill me too."

15The LORD said to him, "Go back the way you came, and go to the Desert of Damascus. When you get there, anoint Hazael king over Aram. 16Also, anoint Jehu son of Nimshi king over Israel, and anoint Elisha son of Shaphat from Abel Meholah to succeed you as prophet. 17Jehu will put to death any who escape the sword of Hazael, and Elisha will put to death any who escape the sword of Jehu. 18Yet I reserve seven thousand in Israel—all whose knees have not bowed down to Baal and all whose mouths have not kissed him."

Let's go to the game tape on this.

1Now

Why is the "now" there? This passage follows the triumphant account of Elijah on Mount Carmel. You may have reminded your hearers of this before reading. And your inflection on this first sentence will indicate that this is following something significant.

Ahab told Jezebel everything Elijah had done and how he had killed all the prophets with the sword.

You are forced here to make a decision. Is Ahab running back like a tattletale? Is he pining? Is he hoping that Jezebel will commiserate or take action?

2So Jezebel sent a messenger to Elijah to say, "May the gods deal with me [*may – the – gods – deal – with – me*] be it ever so severely [*beiteversoseverely*] if by this time tomorrow I do not make <u>your</u> life like that of one of them."

[3]Elijah was afraid [*little pause*] and <u>ran</u> for his life. When
he came to Beersheba in Judah, he left his servant there,
[4]while he himself went a day's journey into the desert.
He came to a broom tree [*little pause*], sat down under
it [*little pause*] and prayed that he might die. "I have had
enough, Lord," he said. "Take my life; I am no better than
my ancestors." [5]Then he lay down under the tree and fell
asleep [*pause*]. All at once an angel touched him and said,
"Get up and eat."

These are some of the tenderest moments in all of Scripture. God is comforting, giving aid to Elijah. There will be time enough for teaching later. Make your tempo and voice inflection match the tenderness.

[6]He looked around, and there by his head was a cake of bread baked over hot coals, and a jar of water. He ate and drank and then lay down again.

Somehow in your pace and tone, you need to capture Elijah's exhaustion.

[7]The angel of the LORD came back a second time and
touched him and said, "Get up and eat, for the journey
is too much for you." [8]So he got up and ate and drank.
Strengthened by that food, he traveled forty days and
forty nights until he reached Horeb, the mountain of
God. [9]There he went into a cave and spent the night. And
the word of the LORD came to him: "What are you doing
here, Elijah?"

This is one of those great questions God asks in Scripture. God in Eden: "Where are you?" God to Cain: "Where is your brother?" Jesus to Martha at Lazarus's death: "Didn't I tell you?" Jesus to Mary in the garden: "Who are you looking for?" Each one demands careful review. What does the text inform us about possible inflection in God's voice? Is he angry? Frustrated? Bemused? Gentle? Once you have made that exegetical decision, conform your voice to your interpretation. I can assure you that God's inflection was not one of boredom or monotone.

> 10 He replied, "I have been very zealous for the LORD God Almighty. The Israelites have rejected your covenant, broken down your altars, and put your prophets to death with the sword. I am the only one left, and now they are trying to kill me too."

Elijah is in a classic self-absorbed, narcissistic frame of mind occasioned by being burned out from adrenal gland exhaustion. He is feeling like he's done a huge thing for God and God's pretty much lacking in an appropriate level of gratitude for Elijah's sacrifice. So a little whining in the voice would seem appropriate, again subject to your exegesis.

> 11 The LORD said, "Go out and stand on the mountain in the presence of the Lord, for the Lord is about to pass by."

Your call on this one. I think it is closer to Moses in the cleft than to a judgment motif. God is doing a wonderful gracious thing here. He could have just jumped to his statement in verse 18 as a retort to Elijah. Instead, he chooses to show Elijah a different side of himself that is not the same one he showed when he rained down fire on the soaked altar before Baal's priests.

> Then a great and powerful wind tore [*"tore" has got to tear through the phrase*] the mountains apart and shattered [*same thing with the shattering*] the rocks before the LORD, but the LORD was not in the wind.

Each of these "But the Lord was not in . . ." statements carries an identical inflection and volume and should be said with a quieter voice, perhaps more slowly than the other words.

> After the wind there was an earthquake, but the LORD was not in the earthquake. 12After the earthquake came a fire, but the LORD was not in the fire. And after the fire came a gentle whisper.

Check your exegesis on this one. Some have suggested that this is not as gentle as many translations have it. But, again, land on your interpretation and make your voice match.

> 13When Elijah heard it, he pulled his cloak over his face and went out and stood at the mouth of the cave. Then a voice said to him, "What are you doing here, Elijah?"

I would match this exactly with how I had read the earlier one.

> 14He replied, "I have been very zealous for the LORD God Almighty. The Israelites have rejected your covenant, broken down your altars, and put your prophets to death with the sword. I am the only one left, and now they are trying to kill me too."

Curious, isn't it, that the demonstration did not cure this point of view? But I imagine he is a little less certain of his feelings now. Think of your little kid who runs inside, having been bopped by the neighborhood bully. When he first tells the story, he can barely catch his breath with his choked-back sobs and frustration. But when you wait a minute and ask him to tell you again, your boy probably gains a bit more control and speaks a bit differently. It is likely Elijah did the same thing here.

> 15The LORD said to him, "Go back the way you came, and go to the Desert of Damascus. When you get there, anoint Hazael king over Aram.
> 16Also, anoint Jehu son of Nimshi king over Israel, and anoint Elisha son of Shaphat from Abel Meholah to succeed you as prophet.
> 17Jehu will put to death any who escape the sword of Hazael, and Elisha will put to death any who escape the sword of Jehu.
> 18Yet I reserve seven thousand in Israel—all whose knees have not bowed down to Baal and all whose mouths have not kissed him."

Bam! Here is the refutation of Elijah's self-absorption. Imagine being able to show your acne-prone, bony, "I'll-never-get-a-date" sixteen-year-old daughter a photograph of her as the twenty-eight-year-old drop-dead beauty you know she will become? That's God's advantage in our lives. Here is God's matter-of-fact declaration of an imperative: "Go," giving Elijah a series of tasks to pull himself out of his fact-less downward spiral. Here God makes his statements of assurance that Elijah is on the winning side. And here God finishes with a Hollywood-style reveal of an army of men who have stayed faithful. Your voice should be strong and resolute and finish with a bit of irony.

So how do we accomplish this approach?

1. Understand the greater context.
2. Choose the appropriate speed.
3. Savor the words.

4. When reading Scripture, visualize the setting in your mind. Your ability to see it will convert over to us. When you read through Elijah's interaction with the angel and then with the Lord, picture the broom tree, the desert, the blue sky, the rocky terrain, and the cave. Feel the heat of the desert sun, the parch in your throat, the pangs of hunger, and fear that Elijah experienced. Experience the wonderful satiation of the angel's meal, that deliciousness of simple food when the hunger is great.
5. Choose carefully which words will receive emphasis. Note the fundamental difference between what you are communicating in the different emphases here:
   a. "*What* are you doing here, Elijah?"
   b. "What are *you* doing here, Elijah?"
   c. "What are you doing *here*, Elijah?"

Which one is textually accurate?

1. Don't look up. Instead, keep your head down and eyes on the page. (See my chapter elsewhere on this.)
2. Enjoy reading Scripture and revel in the privilege.

There are some who may complain that reading in any way that is "not straight" is sacrilege. They would define "not straight" as engaging in any of the above.

These people, however, are missing one simple axiom of life: There is no such thing as "no decision." My computer has hundreds of default settings ranging from the color of the screen to the font on the page to the brightness of the display. I can argue all I want that if I turn on my computer and never change any of those things, I have not made any decisions about them. I would be both wrong and silly.

No decision is itself a decision. "Reading straight," whatever is meant by that term, is itself a product of decisions. Whenever you read Scripture, you are forced to make choices about pace, volume, inflection, and emphasis. Applying "default settings" to any of those aspects of public reading is to make a decision about each of them. Why not make a reasoned and intentional decision about how fast you are going to read, which words call for more attention, or whether this particular dialogue warrants a different tone from that narrative?

Then enjoy the salutary effect on us of hearing the word read well.

Alliteration and Wordplay: Making It Memorable

"If it doesn't fit, you must acquit."

Need I say more? After seven months of trial, scores of witnesses, hundreds of exhibits, thousands of pages of briefs, a billion words put on newsprint, the remainder of how O. J. Simpson would spend his life came down to one little alliterative phrase. Attorney Johnny Cochran's simple genius won freedom for the ex-football star on to back-to-back "it" sounds. The glove didn't fit. So the jury did acquit.

And what's more, if eons from now you remember only one thing about that remarkable chapter in legal social history, it will be that little phrase. *The Boston Globe* remembered.

When Mr. Lucas Hendley Glover won the 109th US Open in four under par, the headline shouted, *GLOVER A GOOD FIT*!

So I ask you, what's the big problem with alliteration?

The oddest criticism of alliteration is that the preacher "forces" words to handle meanings the text does not support. To that I say, if anyone out there is forcing words to handle meaning the text does not support, cut it out. There, solved that problem.

There are twenty-six letters in the English alphabet. If you are not preaching seventeen-point sermons (see my comments above on that bit), then you should be able to find a letter that can handle the demands of two, three, or four words that are reasonably faithful to the text. If you can't, you can surely find three or four sounds that approximate (fit/acquit). Words ending in "ing" do not count.

In addition, that's what the rest of the sermon is for: to elucidate its points. A preacher is not limited to mumbling the three alliterative words over and over again in the vain hope that people will pick up on the meaning and self-complete the rest of the sermon. The preacher is actually allowed to flesh out the points.

Expository Preaching: The Fake Kind

Expository preaching is understood by the unwashed masses (that is, pastors who are too lazy to really work at their sermonic art) to mean choosing any book of the Bible and painstakingly (all puns intended), word by word, verse by verse, and chapter by chapter plod through to the bitter end, calendar be damned.

Worse still, these expository preachers, let's call them Les Expositors, are of the mind-set that simply expositing the

Scripture, telling us what the words mean and what the text means, devoid of illustration and application, is preaching. They couch it with super spiritual erroneous "biblical" argumentation: "Just let the word of God do its work! After all, the word of God is a two-edged sword; it is bread cast upon the waters that doesn't return void. Therefore, there is no need to dress it up or illustrate it as if it needed help."

Oh dear.

Les Expositors fail to see the irony of their logic. Did you notice how God did not tell us that his word is sharp? He used an image rather than just an adjective. He told his hearers and readers of that time that it is as sharp as a two-edged sword. Ever seen or held a two-edged sword? Better yet, ever thought about which you'd rather use to fight a bad guy, a two- or one-edged sword? I'd go for the two-edged over a one-edged sword, because I could slice the bad guy on the way in or out or from the left or right. No matter the direction I swung that weapon, it would cut.

Or have you ever noticed that bread cast on the waters absorbs the water and increases in size? It also floats. If you toss a dry crust into the ocean, it will swell up and bob its way back to you. Apparently, God thinks that humans hear and understand best when truth is conveyed with metaphors, idioms, analogies, parables, similes, comparisons, examples, and illustrations. Jesus seldom stated a proposition without somehow illustrating it.

Allow me to illustrate.

Friend, I ask you: What is the kingdom of heaven?

Try to explain that concept to your dog right now without using the words *partially realized eschatology*. But also don't use any metaphors or similar thingamabobs. Just channel Berkhoff, or any other systematic theologian of your choosing.

Or instead, as you struggle to find the theologically precise definition, give these a shot: The kingdom of heaven is like . . . a mustard seed that is tiny yet grows into the largest of garden plants; a man who sowed good seed in his field but enemies crept in and sowed weeds, so he waited until all were fully grown before separating them; yeast that a woman took and mixed into a large amount of flour; a treasure in a field that a man found and hid again in the field, and then sold everything he owned to buy the field; a pearl of extraordinary value found by a merchant who sold everything to buy it; or a net let down into the lake and pulled in chock-full of good fish and bad, which the fishermen then separated . . .

Jesus, history's greatest preacher, understood the power of the illustration and used it superbly. He knew that explaining the kingdom of heaven in some dry, theological discourse would have tickled the ears of a few Pharisees and then left the rest of us terribly confused with virtually no memory of his words. He also knew that the kingdom of heaven was so multifaceted, and that his hearers' life experiences were sufficiently different, that a variety of metaphors were needed to convey the idea.

Imagine what would happen if we forced Scripture to preach the way Les Expositors preach. Take away the stories. Delete the illustrations. Expunge the applications. Wipe out all the visuals and descriptions. And what have we got? What's left of Scripture? No Genesis. Not much Exodus. We'd have the Ten Commandments, I'll grant them that. We'd keep quite a bit of Leviticus. No Esther. No Ruth. Virtually no Psalms. Hosea's gone. Same with all of Daniel and Revelation. Ezekiel would be squished to nothing. Job, *fuhgettaboutit*. The Gospels would be about nine pages in length. Even Paul's Epistles would be chopped.

God understands that we are full-orbed creatures, endowed with brains with multiple sides, personalities that are varied, experiences that are powerful predictors of how we hear and understand. He knew in preparing the canon that we would need a rich, multifaceted presentation of his truth to reach into the total persons of his people. He expects nothing less of his preachers.

Topical Preaching

I think the occasional topical sermon or sermon series can be a wonderful thing. If you have the pulse of your congregation, you are going to know whether certain issues are of particular interest or needful of addressing. Perhaps marriages are in disarray. Or stewardship is a specific problem. Maybe the congregation has suffered a great deal of loss. Buttressing them up in their faith with a series of sermons focused on what the Bible has to teach us on those matters may be appropriate and beneficial.

But a steady diet of such sermons can have an unintended effect. All preachers have their blind spots that can lead to a failure to ever preach on certain biblical truths. Conversely, all preachers have their favorite topic that can lead to an overemphasis of those topics to the poverty of others. There is good reason for preaching "the whole counsel of God."

My family loves to garden. Each year we'd branch out with new experiments, increase the size of the plot, and try different plants in different conditions. Once, we finished a pretty good season with more tomatoes than we could use or give away. But one crop was a real puzzler. We love Romano pole beans. They produce long flat pods with a superb meaty flavor. We planted dozens of seeds and thinned them to the appropriate spacing. They grew reasonably well until I added MiracleGro. And then did they grow! We had a twelve-foot long, seven-foot high wall of bean plants, three feet thick. The foliage was lush and green, the leaves broad and exceptionally healthy, and the runners aggressive as they spanned out to grab the fencing, the tomato plants, and even us as we walked by.

But as the weeks went by, no beans. No flowers even. So as with many the amateur gardener, I got aggressive with my MiracleGro. And then . . . no beans. So I went to my neighborhood nursery and asked the resident wise man, "What gives?" After hearing my story, he said simply, "You need phosphorus. MiracleGro is great for growing the plant. But it's phosphorus that triggers the production of flowers." One application of a phosphorus rich fertilizer and few weeks later, beans, beans, beans.

Focusing on some biblical truths while neglecting others can lead to that kind of imbalance. Your congregants will be outfitted well to handle marital problems and raising kids, but they may have little appreciation of God's holiness and righteousness. They may have a strong grasp on how to address the moral questions of the hour but may not understand the importance of God's grace in the life of the believer. They may be on fire for evangelism but may not recognize the importance of putting on the full armor of God each morning. Preaching through the Bible one book at a time will give you the best shot at making sure your congregation is being nourished with all the spiritual vitamins, minerals, and food groups Scripture offers.

"I Can't Go up There"

My father and mother were born in Wales into a distinctive early twentieth-century context of preaching when the pulpit was esteemed.

Prior to the rampant rise of secularism and the precipitous fall of religious interest in Wales, going to church was one's assumed Sunday morning and evening task and joy. Well into the last century, Sundays would find the chapels throughout the country packed with the residents of the surrounding villages and valleys. The singing would be robust and tuneful, voices combining to send the richest mixtures of harmonies flowing out of the open windows and past the weed-choked graveyards before soaring heavenward. Hymn singing was so ubiquitous that the order of service became known as a "hymn sandwich," consisting of the welcome, hymn, prayer, hymn, reading, hymn, announcements, hymn, and so on.

Then came the sermon. Before the advent of today's myriad technological distractions, Sunday morning sermons were the high points of the week. The preaching was practically a full-contact sport, with the preacher one of the most revered persons in town. Not because he was the pastor per se. Not because he baptized the young and buried the dead. Not because he wore a collar. Not because he was formally educated (in fact, many were not). No, the preacher was revered because he preached.

The preacher would take a text and explore it carefully, presenting a gracious and awesome God to those gathered beneath the pulpit, and demanding a call to action. Throughout the sermon, the preacher's voice would rise and fall, its inflection holding rapt the attention of the hearers. As the sermon progressed, the preacher could eventually be caught up as by a wind, even by the wind of the Spirit. His words would pour out in what would be heard almost as singing.

But it was not that way every time, and occasionally for the strangest of reasons.

Welsh chapels, which can seat many hundreds, often have balconies built in a "U" that embraces the pulpit and a segregated section below the pulpit of what is called the "big seat." This latter place was a unique element in the chapel construction, akin to the courtroom bar, closing off the pulpit area to the congregation. The pulpit often rose above the "big seat" five or six feet and could be accessed only by a stairway.

Few there were who made that climb. The "big seat" was reserved for the elders of the church and other participants in the service. They all sat there throughout the service and only ascended to the pulpit to play their part. In fact, some—such as the "caller of the tune"—might never ascend and instead simply rose where they were, turned to face the congregation, and sonorously called out the next hymn.

During the hymns and prayers, the preacher would sit down with the elders in the "big seat," worshipping with the congregation. Then, when it came time for the sermon, those gathered would wait with great anticipation for the explication of Scripture, the turns of phrases, the encouragement to the spirit, and, frankly, the fireworks that were about to explode.

But on more than one occasion, in more than one church across Wales, the preacher brought into sharp focus the awesomeness of the task of preaching. When the moment came for him to preach, he would rise from the "big seat," walk solemnly to the foot of the stair, place a hand on the railing and a foot upon the first step, and then stop. Pondering the immense and awful privilege of bringing God's very words to the people gathered and comparing it to a deep sense of his own unworthiness, he would freeze, refusing to ascend the stairs to preach.

In a voice audible only to those around him, he would simply say, "I can't go up there. I can't go up there."

So he wouldn't.

Instead, he would return to his seat, his sermon unpreached. The caller of the tune would hurriedly choose a few hymns to fill the time. Then those gathered would disperse, reminded of the reality of a holy God—One who must be worshipped rightly.

Whatever other analysis we could apply to the event, we would do well to glean at least this: An appropriate and genuine awe about the task should inform us as we preach. Do you see this as simply one other item on your pastoral "to do" list for the week? Is it like teaching a Wednesday night small group Bible study, just with more people and a wireless mic?

Perhaps you have momentarily forgotten that the God you are about to present to these people is the same God who ordered Moses to remove his shoes at the burning bush, who struck down Uriah for the temerity of touching a jostling ark, who dispatched an angel to touch Isaiah's lips with burning coals, who cleared out the temple-turned-marketplace with a whip, who presented Zechariah and his fellow priests with once-in-a-lifetime, highlight-of-their-lives opportunities to serve him in the inner sanctums of his temple, and who by his very essence and name commands a righteous holy fear.

That is the God before whom you are about to present to your congregation. It is his word that you are about to explicate. He is present with you all at that sacred moment. His Spirit is moving about the sanctuary, all-purpose room, storefront, living room, borrowed movie theater, or worship center, ready to take his word into the souls of those listening. And you are about to be his instrument.

Will you get out of your chair with nonchalance? Or will your steps from your seat be made with a passionate excitement, a touch of trepidation at the task that awaits, a hurried

Nehemiah prayer for God's guidance and inspiration, and a holy awe at the task at hand?

Preaching Is the Most Important Aspect of Your Ministry

That may strike you as a pretty controversial statement. But allow me to argue the case. Pound for pound, the most important component of your ministry in your church is what you do for that thirty-minute slot every Sunday morning. Like it or not, a meaningful percentage of your attendees come only on Sunday morning. We have a number of people in our church whose only connection to the church is Sunday morning worship. They don't even attend Sunday school. Thus much of how they experience and view their church is determined by that hour of worship before noon on Sunday. But even for those people who are at the church anytime the lights are on, Sunday morning and your sermon is critical to their growth as Christians.

Preaching can define a church. What is said from the pulpit is, quite fairly, taken as what that particular church believes, how they experience God, what their outlook on life is, what is important to them, how they view the world and their place in it, what their doctrinal underpinnings are, how serious they take their faith, and on and on. Often now, sermons are posted on the church websites. So anyone in the world can, with the click of a mouse, hear what your congregation has heard in each of the last six months of Sundays. Although they will have very little knowledge about your fellowship hour, your youth ministry, your soup kitchen, your physical plant even, they will get a good sense of who you are as a church from those online sermons.

There is nothing else that happens in your church that affects more people than your preaching.

The Counterintuitive Nature of Application

Let's examine the counterintuitive nature of applications.

If a preacher does not apply the truth but rather simply states a truth and hopes for the best, the chances are extremely high that absolutely nobody will apply the truth to his or her own life. If the preacher gets semi-courageous and partly industrious and gives some general even vague examples/applications, a few listeners may be able to see some connection between the sermon and their lives. Those stalwart few may be emboldened to allow the Holy Spirit to change something in their lives.

But if the preacher goes all the way and spells out specific examples of how these truths apply, almost every one of those hearers is going to find that nexus between the truth and praxis. Put another way—and note how counterintuitive this is—the greater the detail of the applications, the easier it will be for all us pew-mates to see the point and start making changes in our lives.

Let's apply that.

Approach 1: Let God apply it.

> So you see, Peter is telling us that people will know that we are Christians by our love. Amen. Now let's sing "Kumbaya" . . .

Percentage of people who will see the light: 1 percent (probably the preacher's spouse).

Approach 2: Give application a half-hearted shot.

> If we care about our coworkers, neighbors, and even relatives, and show them kindness, they'll start to see that there is something different about us. Eventually, they're going to see that we're Christians. They'll see Christ in us because we are loving. Amen. Now, let's sing "We Gather Together" . . .

Percentage of people who will tie the truth to their lives: 17.3+/- percent.

Approach 3: Go nuts and actually work the noggin till it hurts, figuring out a few specific, boots-on-the-ground ways to apply the hard-fought truths.

> So what does this "know we're Christians by our love" mean to you and to me? Next time you're working on a group project at work, stay later, pick up more weight than you need to, then give the credit to the group or highlight someone else's idea when you make the presentation to your boss. That's love. Or next time you're talking with the neighborhood folks and someone starts bad-talking an absent neighbor, step in and gently defend her, but in a way that is not cross or annoying. That's love. Or when people complain about Christians, have a story ready to tell of some sister from church who showed you how much she cared about you when you had a baby by bringing three hot home-cooked meals including linen napkins and a package of Andes Crème de Menthe thin mints. That's love. Or if you're at Northridge High School and see some kid getting bullied, use

> up some of your political capital and quietly rescue the kid and talk him through to the other side of the pain and loneliness. That's love. They'll know we are Christians by our love. By our love. Not first by our anger at societal wrongs. But by our love. Not first by our brilliant apologetics that destroy the pillars of their unbelief. But by our love. Not first by seeing us sanctimoniously drive to church on Sunday while they clip their hedges. But by our love. By our love. By our love. Amen. Now let's sing that Rich Mullins song, "A Love That Knows No Bounds" . . .

Percentage of people who will be motivated to act on the truths: 92 percent (the rest are still stuck back on the notion of giving credit for their hard work to someone else and are hating the idea).

Breaking the Stained-Glass Ceiling

I've got a good friend who is off-the-charts smart. By now, she is a brilliant New Testament scholar delving into and teaching the nuances of the original languages in ways that will benefit the coming generation of preachers.

She herself has received the occasional invitation to preach. And a few years ago, she had history thrust upon her. She had been asked to preach at an evening "contemporary" service of a large historic metropolitan church on whose staff she served at the time. This was unusual, because women generally were not invited to preach in this particular pulpit. But the evening service was packed with collegians and graduate students, and so perhaps the leadership felt that no ruckus would be raised.

Not that she needed it with any urgency, but she asked me to run through her sermon. We did the normal amount of tweaking illustrations, emphasizing applications, and making sure that the sermon had good flow.

Some preachers bring more of a lecturing approach to their preaching. The content may be solid, but the delivery can lack the power and pacing that sets preaching apart. The key is to move from that teaching mode to a preaching mode. And with a few adjustments, my friend made that shift. I attended that evening service and enjoyed an excellent sermon.

But history would happen a week later. That Sunday afternoon, we received an excited call from my friend. The morning's guest preacher had taken ill in the middle of the first of two morning worship services. No elder was prepared to preach. There was no other pastor there. Nobody had a sermon fired up and ready to go. Except for my pal. This was the classic "lead actor has laryngitis" or "starting pitcher tears rotator cuff in shower on game day" scenario. The elders gave her the nod, and my friend grabbed her fresh sermon notes and went where God had called her.

The only other woman to have ever taken that pulpit on a Sunday morning in historical memory had been Corrie Ten Boom, and she did not preach. But our intrepid preacher preached, proclaiming God's word to a waiting congregation.

Start Correctly

My Welsh roots have given me the opportunity to conduct hymn-singing festivals across the country. The Welsh have a genetic love for hymns and harmony, sometimes most prominently demonstrated by beer-addled compatriots singing in the stands at a rugby match.

The distinctive of the Welsh hymn-sing is that there is no audience, as the entire congregation is the choir and sits and sings in four-part harmony. Over the years, I have had the chance to conduct congregations from twenty-five to fifteen hundred strong. One of the keys to harnessing a group of fifteen hundred singers who have never sung together, and in the course of an afternoon create a choir out of them, is to gain control. Their trust and confidence in the conductor establishes that control.

The programs are generally structured the same. There will usually be four sets of three to four hymns each. As the invited conductor, my job is to take this rather unwieldy, occasionally unruly, and by definition, completely unpracticed crowd of singers, and transform them into a choir. In less than twelve hymns.

I've figured out how to do it before even a single note is sung. Here's how.

We humans have internal timepieces, little gut clocks that tell us automatically how much time should be between events. We press an elevator button, and there is a short range of how long our clock will allow us to wait before we begin to complain. We put out our hand to greet someone, and there is an appropriate timeframe for that other person to reciprocate with her hand. Too quick and we will think she was trying to hit us. Too slow and we will be insulted. When we answer the phone and say hello, we have a precise amount of time within which we expect to hear a response. If that response is delayed, we know that we have a telemarketer or a creep on the other end of the line.

Well, the same is true for the space of time after an organ plays the introduction to a hymn and the time everyone expects to begin singing. At each hymn-singing festival, I cue the organ and conduct the organist through the introduction to the first hymn. Someone may have introduced me as the event's conductor, but I will not have uttered a word to anyone. As the organist finishes the introduction, I motion for everyone to stand. The organist stops playing and I raise my arms.

And I wait.

Everyone's internal clock alarm goes off, and invariably someone will begin singing. But I have given no downbeat of the conductor's baton. I am frozen. I look with slight sternness at the congregation, wait just a brief moment more, and then dive into the hymn.

They will not look away from me again for the rest of the festival.

Dollars to donuts the members of your congregation have that internal clock that tells them exactly how much time there should be between the end of the sermon-preparatory hymn and when you are supposed to start preaching. They will be arranging their bulletins, shushing their children, crossing their legs, finding their pens, and knowing, just knowing that you will begin your sermon when their clocks go off.

But don't start. Wait. Wait just long enough to mess up the majority of the clocks. Then they'll be with you from the start.

Don't Avoid the Tough Questions in a Text

Sooner rather than later, every preacher will run up against tough questions in the text. You must address them, even if it is to say, "Don't have a clue."

But you should have at least a clue. Give us a sense of the options. Christ preached to the spirits in prison. When?

Was that back in the days of Noah? Was it after his resurrection? Was he successful? What was his sermon about? Of course, the text is not going to answer all the questions, but give us a sense of your struggle. The fact that you had to work hard at understanding it—and even may not have a definitive opinion—helps convey a sense of the richness of God's word. Be more afraid of the effect on us of skipping over the tough verses than of showing us your sweat.

There are plenty of aids to give you that clue. Unshelf an armful of commentaries. Check out *Hard Sayings of the Bible* by Walter C. Kaiser Jr. et al. (IVP, 1996). You can surely find scholars who have included your text in their analysis of the really thorny passages of Scripture. Call your old biblical professor. Phone a friend. Use a lifeline. Pray and meditate on the passage.

What are the dangers of skipping merrily over the text? First, you will be teaching us to be lazy in our own study. You will make us less brave and adventurous in our private reading of Scripture. If it's a hard one for you, it's probably near impossible for us. If you have one hundred problem texts, we've got one thousand. If you don't need to wrestle with them, then why should we?

Second, you will be communicating that parts of God's Scripture are actually not ordained for teaching because they're just too tough to understand. So, we'll essentially learn to delete the gnarly bits of the Bible. That would not be a good thing.

Finally, you will not be preaching "the whole counsel of God." Buried in the confusing texts are a great many nuggets that, when taken in the whole context of Scripture in the hands of the Holy Spirit, will speak to our souls in ways that may be beyond conscious understanding. Don't cheat us out of those pieces of gold.

Preaching Is Not Anything Else

Preaching is not lecturing.
Preaching is not teaching.
Preaching is not conversation.
Preaching is not soliloquizing.
Preaching is most decidedly not acting.
Preaching is not entertainment.
Preaching is not argument.
Preaching is not a sales presentation.
Preaching is not performance art.

Preaching is neither an opening statement nor a closing argument.

Although it may have elements of all of the above (with the exception of acting), in the end . . .

Preaching is preaching.

"Wizard of Ahhs"

I live in the politically storied Commonwealth of Massachusetts. We boast some of the most important figures in United States political history: Governor John Winthrop, John Adams, John Quincy Adams, Tip O'Neill, and the entire Kennedy clan. Perhaps the most powerful senator in the United States Senate in the twentieth century was Ted Kennedy. Whatever side of the political game you took, Senator Kennedy was a fascinating man. Having worked elbow to elbow with decades of presidents, senators, representatives, and world leaders, he was a commanding force when pursuing his political agenda.

As a Kennedy, he was accompanied by a high expectation that he would excite the masses with his oratory. His brother the president was a very effective public speaker. And on occasion, Senator Kennedy thrilled his supporters with classic soaring Kennedy rhetoric. But not always.

One of our most popular Boston drive-time talk radio hosts, Howie Carr, did not include himself in the ranks of major Kennedy fans. Instead, he created a regular bit for his listeners called "The Wizard of Ahhs." Mr. Carr gave the rules of the game essentially as follows: "I'm going to play a taped excerpt from a recent Senator Kennedy speech. Count how many 'ahhs' the Senator says: 'ahhhhhh' is one; 'ah, ah' is two; I am the final arbiter. This one is twenty-three seconds long. Three, two, one, go!"

> The, ah, program, ah, has with it some, ah, ah, significant, ah, ah, ah, advantages that we ah, aaahh-rrr, just, ahhhhh, beginning to, ah, see.

The listeners then plugged up the phone lines. "Nine, Howie!" Buzzer. "Six, Howie!" Buzzer. "Eleven, Howie!" Buzzer. "Ten, Howie!" Ding ding ding, a winner! Usually, the prize was a gift certificate to Bickford's Family Restaurant, plus the satisfaction of a good laugh.

Verbal pauses can take a multiple of forms. They include any word, guttural sound, or phrase inserted into speech that carry with them no content or meaning. The most common are the "ahhs," "uhhs," and "umms." They also include "you know," "to be honest with you," "well," "I mean," and the absolutely infernal "like." Then there are some even longer ones that truly make no sense. I know one man who inserts the phrase "by all means" into a conversation twice a minute in a way that carries no connection at all to the content of his message. Other folks lose no opportunity, no matter the hour, to jam in "at the end of the day."

I remember one meal in an award-winning restaurant where the food was coddled and the wallet was damaged. The waiters described what we were about to eat using the following verbal pause nugget: "We have here the chef's signature dish, braised lamb with a demi-glace port and fennel seed reduction, *if you will*, pomme du terre with mounded asparagus points, *if you will*, finished with a rosemary olio carli, *if you will*." Gee thanks, given that I just shelled out a week's wages for this entrée, I THINK I WILL!

In my morning devotions, I enjoy using a collection of Puritan prayers, *The Valley of Vision*. I have been really impressed by the way that these dead people prayed without using the word *just*. Judging by today's corporate prayers, it seems that God would not understand us if we omitted *just* from every other sentence. "Lord, we, just, pray this morning, that you would, just, give us your blessing. We, just, thank you for being you."

Sometimes people will go for the maximum verbal pausing to get the verbal engine revved up.

> Bo: So Slim, what are you thinking of doing this weekend?
>
> Slim: Ahh, well, I mean, you know, I'm going to, like, uh, clean out my car.

In the pulpit, the verbal pauses are hardly ever your friend. They proclaim your uncertainty about what you are trying to say. They interrupt the flow of your words. They annoy. They consume valuable time. They become oral speed bumps needlessly slowing down your delivery. They, uh, at the end of the day, umm, just, uh, make it, like, hard, to, ah, listen, you know, attentively, if you know what I mean.

Now you might say that you have heard some of the best preachers alive today, and you've heard them using verbal pauses. Some of these preachers even use them as a trademark. So why can't you? To that I suggest we talk about US Open Champion Jim Furyk and his golf swing. Golf commentator David Feherty has been widely quoted describing the swing as "an octopus falling out of a tree." Unlike the fluid swings of Rory McIlroy, Fred Couples, and hundreds of other professional golfers, Furyk's swing is an odd loop. For a game where a smooth, pleasing swing appears to be an absolute requirement, Furyk violates a few parts of that tenet. You say, why can't I swing like Furyk? If your golf ball ends up where Furyk's does—in the middle of the fairway, on the green, in the hole—then swing away with all your awkward hiccups. My guess, though, is that your swing provides the same location results as mine—namely, in the woods, in the rough, in the bunker, on the green, across the green, back across the green, near the hole. Pick up and move on. We ain't no Furyk. Dump the verbal pauses.

Why Are You Preaching That Passage to This Congregation on This Particular Day?

I often enjoy the honor of working with pastors on their preaching. In anticipation of one such meeting, a pastor sent me a set of his most recent sermon audio recordings. I popped in the first sermon to hear a sermon on one of David's psalms. "Today we continue our series in the Psalms," I heard him tell his congregation as he began his sermon. The next week's sermon was from another psalm. "We're continuing our series in the psalms," he began. Finally, the third week's sermon contained an introduction with the long-awaited explanation of why we were in the Psalms. "We're continuing our series in the Psalms, because I've been reading a book on the Psalms in my private devotions. The book I'm reading is a long book, so I don't know how long we'll be in the Psalms. Probably not as long as my devotions. But we'll see."

Now let's think about what he is unwittingly telling his congregation.

> "I really have no strategy here for where I'm trying to take you. I'm not particularly aware of your spiritual needs. What I speak about on Sunday morning is essentially a matter of pure, random coincidence. My choices of sermon texts owe more to chaos theory than intelligent design. Who knows where we'll be in a month. But please continue to show up with a vague sense of hope that something I'll say will be of some use to you."

Not a terribly inspiring rationale for the choice of sermon series.

If you are going to preach a sermon, then you are going to have to choose a biblical text. If you choose a biblical text, then you are going to have to use some sort of decision-making process. What is that process? Do you choose based on whim? Based on what is interesting to you? Based on "what God's been doing in my life"? Based on what your pulpit hero has been preaching on the radio?

Even if your goal is simply to preach the entire canon to your congregation, you will have to decide which books to tackle first and the order of any after them. Unless you are going to be at this church for the next five or six decades, you are probably not going to cover every verse in the Bible.

So what are you trying to do with your congregation? Where are you taking them? What are you feeding them? Do they need to increase their intimacy with Jesus and know him as their Lord and friend? Preach from a Gospel. In recent years, has your congregation been marked by discord or a lack of Christian charity? Pick Corinthians or Philippians. Have you not focused enough recently on the wonder of God and his attributes? Now preach from the Psalms and pick them well. Do you need to develop a better understanding of God's covenant promises and his zeal to pick and protect a people? Choose anything from the Old Testament. Does your congregation have a developed theological understanding of Christ? Preach from Colossians or Hebrews. Does the congregation have a good idea what life is all about? Preach Genesis 1–3 for a couple of months and throw in an Ecclesiastes chapter or two. Do they need a heavenly perspective? Tackle Revelation.

Keep a flexibility to address particular spiritual needs or events in the life of the congregation. But have a plan that extends out beyond the next week, or even six months. Have a plan, and be willing to change it as needed. By doing so, you will be assured of covering the Bible in a comprehensive manner. And we, your congregation, will rest secure knowing that your preaching has purpose. We will come with greater expectation and understanding each week, knowing that our knowledge and love for God is being encouraged and built in a thoughtful way.

Be intentional about what you preach, and why you preach what you preach.

Physical Preparation (Part 2)

I always stretch out before I speak in a public setting. I do essentially the same routine as I have been doing for thirty years before I go out for a run or a workout. I stretch the quads, hamstrings, and calves, the arms, torso, and neck. That way, I can be sure that I will have my full range of motion, that my muscles will not cramp up and that my blood is flowing.

Develop your own routine. Do a few sit-ups or pushups. Walk around your campus or down the block. Take a few deep breaths. Look up to the sky. Jump in place. Jog a hundred yards. Swing your arms like a windmill. Eat a Fig Newton.

There is no escaping that your body is involved in your preaching. Don't surprise it at 11:23 on Sunday morning by forcing it to stand and to speak without giving it some advance warning and preparation.

Know the Jargon

My brother-in-law, Kevin, is a fine preacher. A careful student of Scripture, he preaches with infectious enthusiasm and with a creative mind. He also has that wonderful ability to connect with any kind of person, any kind of congregation.

Born in Britain, on his first visit to the United States, he spoke to a congregation consisting of about five hundred Americans and three Welshmen. He was holding forth with a presentation on the 1904 Welsh Revival replete with overhead slides. (Imagine what revivalist Evan Roberts could have done during that time if he'd had this technology! More on that below.) As Kevin began speaking about one eminent preacher, a sepia photograph of the man (complete with hair circa 1904 and a big bushy mustache) filled the projection screen behind him. In his customary animated style, Kevin quipped to the congregation, "Oh, I love his tush—I wish I could have a tush like that."

Unknown to his stunned American audience, "tush" is British short for mustache. Equally and blissfully unknown to our bold Welsh preacher, "tush" is American short for derriere, bum, backside, etc. And worse, "tush" is never American short for mustache. The other three Brits knew both of these things, and it was all they could do to stay on their tushes in the sanctuary.

Preach to the Cows

As a doctoral student in Edinburgh, my father would take long afternoon walks to think, ponder, and meditate. His route took him out into the Scottish countryside where he would practice preaching his sermons to the cows in the fields. It was there that he developed the ability to "throw" his voice and later fill large halls unassisted by a microphone. Richard Burton did the same thing with Shakespeare to the sheep on the hills of Wales. And he got to marry Elizabeth Taylor. Twice.

The Mic Is Your Friend

Mr. Microphone is your buddy. But sometimes he leaves for a break. Sometimes he gets tired and raspy and gives you all kinds of feedback, none of it positive. Sometimes he echoes. Sometimes airline pilots flying overhead inhabit his body. So you need to be prepared to go solo, au naturale.

If you have a preacher's voice, then you will be able to preach to just about any room without a microphone. The preacher's voice starts in the diaphragm. It used to beat the heck out of me what that meant. I think I've figured it out. Give this a shot: with about one-third of a lungful of air, try speaking from the middle of your throat. Now take a deep full breath of air and shift the voice production down to your belly. You should sense an immediate improvement in the volume and control. That's preaching from the diaphragm.

Before you try preaching mic-less, make sure you have confirmed with someone outside of your own brain that you can successfully speak to fill a large room. Otherwise, you may join the ranks of the "shared mic disaster" that typically arises at a "town meeting" type event. This is when people are invited to speak to the gathered masses using a mic set in a stand in the front of the hall. One after the other, they dutifully, and usually awkwardly, approach the microphone and say their piece. Short ones never bother to adjust the stand down, and instead crane their mouths upwards like little birds waiting for a bit of worm from the mommy bird. The mic usually does not oblige. Tall participants stoop down, down, and down to it, and then peer at us all through their eyebrows, bobbing and tilting their heads like Cirque du Soleil contortionists as they make their points.

But then comes the fellow who fancies himself a "public speaker." Having witnessed his lesser orators' troubles with the mic but believing the accoutrement to be beneath his dignity, he strides to the front and, with what is typically best described as disdain, pushes the mic aside and bellows, "Can everyone hear me?" Now of course we all nod affirmatively, because he just bellowed the words "Can everyone hear me?" Yup, we sure can hear you. Phew, we think to ourselves. Finally, someone we can hear. Then, most unfortunately, Mr. Orator proceeds to mumble as if he's in a booth at a Denny's for a meeting with a hit man over a Super Slam breakfast.

If you're going to go without the mic, make sure you are throwing your voice to the usher sleeping in the foyer. That way everyone in between will be the delighted beneficiary of your words. Otherwise, stick with the mic.

If you do, remember that there is an art to using the microphone.

First of all, watch those "plosives"—the *p's* and *t's* that eventually will feel like small woodpeckers on your listeners' foreheads. Take care not to shout into your microphone. Make sure to adjust it to your height. Unless you have the voice of an angel, have the sound techies cut off your portable mic before you start singing that hymn. And please make sure that those same techies turn that little guy on before you start speaking again, not three and half words into your prayer/Scripture/sermon.

On the whole, the preacher's world is better off with microphones. The possibilities for modifying your dynamics are measurably enhanced. Your urgent voice gains power. Your whispers can comfort or hiss as you wish. Your emphasized words can pop with an explosiveness that the natural human voice usually lacks. Your normal speaking voice can easily reach the far corners of the room. For most of us, those are not altogether bad advantages.

Get a Critic

I enjoy gourmet food and fine dining. As long as I can go get a burger later, I even enjoy fussy foods. Dishes that take the waiter as long to describe as they take to eat can only inspire. "This is the chef's complementary *amuse bouche*, which is a savory sesame profiterole with Tuscany oregano and smoked kangaroo shavings." Gimme two of them bad boys, Garçon.

But don't ask me to tell you why I like or don't like a particular dish. My observations would be limited to: "This is cooked perfectly," or "What a delicious, succulent piece of meat," or if I'm really on my game, "There seems to be a good deal of garlic in this dish."

You will not find me able to wax eloquently about how the acidic nature of the mango interacts well with the woody flavor of the venison such and such. Or how this particular seasoning of tarragon cooperates perfectly with that anise. No, at the end of the day, I am going to tell you whether I thought the meal was yummy or not.

That is, like it or not, how most people are with preaching. They know whether they liked it or not. But they can't tell you much more than that. Many people don't even think in broad categories about preaching. They would not leave thinking, "That preacher really was able to bring me to the foot of God's throne," or "He brought home some significant nuances from that text that I haven't seen before."

Very few in your congregation will be able to analyze your sermon in great depth or sophistication. But although most of them would agree that they are not qualified food critics, they often fancy themselves good preaching critics.

I love listening to commentator and former NFL quarterback Tony Romo when watching a football game. While it is my wife who gave me a spectator's love of the game, commentators like Romo give me an understanding of it. I will watch a play and see a quarterback take the ball, stand for a few seconds, and unleash a pass to a streaking player. Romo will then explain what he saw. White circles will fill the screen as he describes what the other twenty players were doing as the play unfolded. "This fullback hesitated for a moment to fool his defender. That lineman pushed to his right just before he ducked down to his left. This receiver exploded off the line of scrimmage at full speed, taking two defenders with him." And each of the moves has a name and, for the aficionados, a history and a purpose.

You need a Tony Romo. You need a fellow chef. You need someone in your life who can review your preaching and explain things you cannot see. Someone who can intelligently articulate why some things you do are so effective and why others could be improved. Even John Grisham has an editor and Roger Federer, the greatest tennis player ever, has a coach.

It could be your old seminary professor, a trusted member in your church, or a fellow pastor from across town, but get someone to break down the game tape from time to time.

Some Thoughts for the Spouses

Husband or wife, if your spouse preaches, half of you are in the pulpit on a Sunday morning.

You have seen that preaching well is an extremely demanding task. It requires a great deal of preparation. It also requires significant concentration during the sermon itself.

The more you can do to free up your preacher spouse to prepare and then to concentrate, the better he or she will preach.

Try to create the appropriate spiritual environment each Sunday morning. See if you can keep the kids from fighting. Try to keep yourself from fighting with your preacher spouse. Remember that this is a spiritual battle in which you are participating. Stay on the same side together.

When all is said and done and it's dinner time after church, say happy things only. Have a rule together that any critique and even the most innocuous suggestion need to be reserved at least until Monday. Since you have your entire lives together, be sparing in any criticism from week to week. Your spouse needs your support and cheerleading more than criticism. This is particularly true if he or she has another coach or someone to analyze the sermons.

Having said that, often during my father's sermons (about thirty minutes in) my mother would casually hold her left arm across her chest and gently grasp her wristwatch with her right hand. Her motion was invisible to anyone else, but for my father the gesture was a subtle reminder: "ENOUGH ALREADY. WRAP IT UP, DARLING." If at the end of his life he had one regret about his preaching, it was that he didn't take her advice about sermon length often enough.

"If You Haven't Struck Oil in Twenty-Five Minutes, Stop Boring"

I'm not sure there is anyone who can keep a modern, twenty-first-century American congregation concentrating for fifty minutes. Thirty minutes is probably an outside stretch.

In my first jury trial, I had the judge tell me and the opposing counsel that jurors stop listening to a witness after twenty minutes. That's right, twenty minutes. The judge was indeed correct. Of course, in a lengthy trial, they will tune back in from time to time and, hopefully, at least a few of the twelve will be listening at any given time. But the individual listener's attention span is limited.

"You're kidding!" you'll tell me. "There is no way I can say all that I need to in thirty minutes." To that I say, "Try twenty-five minutes instead." That is plenty of time to develop the "big idea" if that is your philosophy. It is also plenty of time to develop three points, at six to seven minutes each point.

There are still exceptions to that rule. Often on the ride home after church, my wife and I listen to one pastor on the radio who preaches for forty-five minutes and we are never bored. He knows to pack his sermons with contemporary references and challenges to action and application. His interpretations of Scripture are solid but somehow fresh. He is also smarter than most of us. So he can get away with forty-five minute sermons. The rest of us should cut that by a third.

Get Them on Their Feet

Never preach to a congregation that has been sitting for more than ten minutes. They have already used up precious reserves of deliberation. Stick in a hymn or praise song just before the sermon. Although there are plenty of much more spiritual reasons why singing is a good thing as a preparation for worship, allowing the congregation to get their blood circulating and move their limbs a bit will pay dividends later in their powers of concentration.

If you are a visiting preacher with no control over the order of service, have the congregation stand for the reading of God's word just before you preach. If they are not used to that, it might freak them out a bit, but they'll be all the more ready to listen just to see what other unexpected thing you might say or do.

A Wasp up the Trousers

My father once had a wasp fly up his suit trouser leg in the middle of his sermon. Ours is not to question why. Ours is to squish the bug until he dies. Unfortunately, the reason my father was sure it was a wasp because in its frustration at failing its undisclosed quest, the angry insect stung my father on the leg. My father, without stopping his preaching, reached down and crushed the wasp against his leg. He went on to complete his sermon without further incident. He also made no mention of the wasp, its journey, or its ultimate end.

There was no advantage to his sermon in pointing out to the congregation that a wasp had just flown up his trousers and stung him. The congregation would have spent the rest of the sermon wondering if my father was allergic and would swell up in anaphylactic shock, pondering exactly where it had stung him, or questioning whether it was actually dead or would it sting again somewhere worse. So nothing would be gained by disclosing to the congregation the event, painful as it was. Had there been some advantage, however, I'm pretty sure he would have taken it.

Communion

Is there anything better than a great Communion service? All the textures of our Christian walk are present. The almost palpable presence of Christ, remorse, forgiveness, redemption, sobriety, joy, the sacrifice seen from the viewpoint of success, peace, reconciliation, strength for today, grace and hope for tomorrow, and a hundred more facets of what it is to know Christ. It's the *Lord's* Table. We're all just guests. But honored, welcomed ones. All of that wrapped into eight or nine minutes of quietude.

How can you increase the odds that Communion at your church will be more meaningful? Certainly, praying for your congregation helps. Making sure that your recitation of the order of the Communion service is not rote will also advance the cause. Having music that enhances the meditative nature is great.

But there is one thing overlooked by many preachers.

Communion should not come as a surprise. In most orders of service, Communion follows the sermon. And in most of those, Communion seems like an awkward appendage tacked on to the back of the service like a camel's hump. The ceremony is probably beneficial for some reason, but just what is not so easily intuited. Too often we find ourselves taking Communion as if it were a stand-alone hiccup in the service, a once-a-month necessity without connection to anything else that has gone on before or will follow.

Therefore, make sure that your sermon leads the congregation into Communion. Mention in your sermon some link to the spiritual feast that is about to be spread before them. Say anything, such as, "Shortly, we will be participating in that grace of Christ as we take Communion together." Look for connections between your passage and Communion, between an illustration and Communion, between an application and Communion, between one of your points and Communion. Your preaching should be Christocentric every Sunday. Communion is nothing if not Christocentric. Then, as you administer the sacrament, harken back to what you just preached to bind it into Communion.

After a sermon on anxiety:

> Do you find yourself anxious? This sacrament, with these elements, is where you begin today to find comfort and a calming of the storms of anxiety as we commune with our Lord at his table.

After a sermon on sin:

> Where is forgiveness of sin? Here in front of us we see in a tangible fashion the beating heart of forgiveness. This is where we come face to face with a redeeming Lord.

After a sermon on tithing:

> It's so much easier to give money back to God when we remember that he loved us in this way, that he gave us his Son to die for us.

Because Jesus is relevant to anything you preach and we experience, tying your sermon to Communion will be a simple matter.

No Objection to Objects

Have you ever seen a Samurai sword in a pulpit? A piece of a meteorite? A doll? A prayer shawl from Israel? A walking stick? A dollar bill? A piece of olive wood? A remote-controlled airplane? If you had, you'd remember it today.

You can, and should, strive to find great illustrations. You can, and should, work on the wording and phrasing to capture the best and most poetic way to develop the illustration. You can, and should, work through eliminating the unnecessary details in the description while retaining the essential elements.

Or you can just pull Grandpa's ashes off the mantelpiece and take him into the pulpit with you.

Sometimes the best way to present an object lesson is with an object. I don't think there is *anything* as effective in getting people to listen as pulling your illustrative object from under the pulpit. It doesn't matter if precious congregants are reading a newspaper surreptitiously, planning their dinner menu behind their foreheads, worrying about their stock portfolios in their cerebral cortexes, wondering how "they" got the loudspeakers to hang from the ceiling like that, getting excited about playing flag football that afternoon, or just staring catatonically at the trees swaying outside as they all flatline their way to the end of your sermon. If you pull out a spent WWII artillery shell, they're all going to snap their heads vertical.

When using an object, keep a couple of things in mind. First, and this is essential, keep the item hidden from everyone until the appointed time for its reveal. A good lump of the beneficial effect is in the surprise. If your Hank Aaron autographed hickory baseball bat is sitting on top of the pulpit throughout your sermon, nobody will be listening to you until you use it. Worse, they'll be using most of their brainpower trying to figure out when you are going to grab it and what it's supposed to illustrate.

Second, use items sparingly. There is a comedian named Carrot Top who has made a decent living with prop comedy (not all of it clean, so be cautious!). He understands the power of a physical object. He runs around the stage at the Luxor in Las Vegas, randomly pulling out props and disposing of them with one-liners. Often the words are unnecessary as the item communicates all the humor and zaniness needed. His comedy style is a high-octane, rapid-fire frenzy with a "something-for-everyone" approach to nailing his audience. It all works for folks in Vegas after an evening of losing money at blackjack and stuffing themselves at the $9.99 all-you-can-eat buffet. But dozens of props are not the recipe for success in the pulpit where edification, not entertainment, is the goal.

Just remember that the point of the object is the point, not the object.

Third, where possible and where its size is not intentional, try to bring something large enough for the congregation to see. If your image is being broadcast to your right and left on a Jumbotron, then don't worry about this principle. But for the rest of us, the illustration will work best if we can make out some level of detail. Of course, you should describe the object as you hold it, no matter how large or small. "I'm holding here a baseball card, and not just any baseball card but a mint condition T206 Honus Wagner that I found in a box of baseball cards I just bought last week at a yard sale for four bucks." Or "Here's a satellite earth shot of our church in a five-mile radius. How many people do you know who live in the apartment buildings and houses appearing in this picture?"

By the way, don't ask, "Can everyone see this?" What are you going to do differently if someone from the back shouts "No!"?

Preach Christ

Paul kept it real simple. He tells the believers in Colossae that there was a mystery that was hidden for ages and generations. It turns out that the mystery was a lode of glorious riches. Centuries of human living and history passed, and people did not "get it." God had kept it hidden. Then, *kaboom*, God intrudes in the flesh! After millennia of waiting, men and women could hold God's hand in the human form of Jesus. And then that intimacy, that immediacy, became permanent. It is "Christ in you," the hope of glory. Of all the church history, philosophy, theology, sociology, anthropology, psychology, ichthyology, and any other "ology" options that you want to throw in there, it is Christ that Paul preaches.

As a family, we love telling each other stories about our days. My wife, Nina, and I catch up throughout the day and then conduct a far more comprehensive evaluation of the goings-on after dinner. My mother has lived with us for over two decades now. One of our fondest times of the day is to gather with her in the late evening to chat. If something exciting or fun happened during the past twelve hours, we warn each other not to talk about it until we're all together! If someone leaves the room to get a glass of milk, they caution the others to "talk about boring stuff" until he or she returns. Our kids caught on to the excitement of chatting and fellowship to the point that they dissolve into weepy puddles if one of us preempts the telling of "their" stories.

You the preacher get to tell *the* Story. Week after week from a thousand different angles out of ten thousand different texts, you have the privilege of letting us in on this secret, the mystery for all the ages. The complications, excitements, vicissitudes, triumphs, uncertainties, joys, anxieties, and rewards of life find their crux point, their secret decoder ring, their interpretive lens, their whole purpose and explanation *in Christ*. Scripture is understood backwards by grasping that God always intended to send Christ. Everything that needs to make sense does so once we *get Christ*.

Plenty has been written on the redemptive historical approach to preaching, where we see Old Testament passages as foreshadowing Christ and we understand all of Scripture as pointing to his coming to redeem us. Some preachers demur from seeing Christ in every passage of the Bible. Fair enough. My intention is not to impose upon all of us the necessity of preaching from one school of thought. But whatever your understanding is of the matter, your sermons need to preach Christ in some way. As you do, you and we will see God's handprints throughout the history of his people leading them to Christ.

Don't Be Afraid of Big Words

Words are your tools of trade. Develop your vocabulary. Do not be afraid to use big words where appropriate. But here's the trick: Follow the word immediately with a more common synonym. "Think of this, the disciples have been fishing all night and as they approach the shore, what a *serendipity* awaits them, what a surprise, what an unexpected turn of events, as Jesus is there with a breakfast hot and ready."

You might ask, "Isn't that tautological rhetoric?"

To which I say, "Oh, it's not a tautology. This is no endless repetition without purpose. I'm not saying the same thing over and over again pointlessly." Instead, I am making full use of the English language and making sure I bring my listeners along with me. For the few of you who haven't used the word *tautology* lately, you grasped the meaning of the word by the end of the paragraph.

Martin Lloyd-Jones used this technique of repetition to great effect. He would restate his point three or four different ways, one immediately after the other. He was known to preach for over an hour, and I've often thought that he could have shortened his sermons to about seventeen minutes had he not repeated himself.

And now for some completely random selections of Lloyd-Jones from the first page I opened (page 66) from his book *Life in the Spirit in Marriage, Home, and Work: An Exposition of Ephesians 5:18–6:9* (Baker, 1973). Here is Lloyd-Jones on ecumenism and Ephesians 5:21 on submitting to one another out of reverence for Christ:

> This text is being abused in that way today. . . . Do you imagine that the Apostle Paul in this verse is preaching

> peace at any price, and saying that a man should ride lightly and loosely to the truth, and that he should be pliable and accommodating and compromising as regards doctrine? Is he teaching a false humility here? Is he saying that loyalty to institutional Christianity comes before everything, and that a man must put his opinions on one side and conform to the general line and say what everybody else is saying? Does the Apostle's teaching run on those lines?

One of my favorite William F. Buckley Jr. quotes was his response to criticism of his use of language: "I am lapidary but not eristic when I use big words." Now come on, is that not priceless! Why can't we slide "lapidary" or "eristic" into a sentence once in a while? When I first read that remark, I had some vague notion of what "lapidary" meant but no idea on "eristic." My life is better now for having explored the words.

You may be remonstrating, objecting, balking, complaining, disapproving, or otherwise protesting my point here. I say, demur at will. Your reasoned opposition is probably based on a perceived contradiction. You are recalling that my stated main purpose in writing this book is to encourage the addition of things that will make it more likely that your preaching will be understood and the deletion of those things that detract from comprehension.

You may wonder whether big words, at first blush, create an impediment to the message reaching the person in the pew. Words are your tools of trade. Undoubtedly, you can handle most simple tasks around the house with a hammer, pair of pliers, and a screwdriver with a reversible Phillips and flathead. But every once in a while, you'll need that hex wrench or awl, or those pin-nose pliers. And occasionally, nothing but an oil-filter wrench will do.

Four Words

What do you want us to *know*, *feel*, *do*, or *be* as a result of your sermon this coming Sunday?

Positive Is the Word for Your Family

If you are parenting, your family may be a treasure trove of effective illustrations. Between the four walls of your home exists a microcosm of everything we experience daily. You are dealing with, enjoying, fighting for, and exulting in marriage. You are delighting in, watching over, caring for, and nurturing a family from cradle to car to curfew to college commencement. You are caring for and burying aged relatives. All from that home base. What an endless source of illustrations.

There is, however, an inviolable principle to apply here. You must never use your spouse or your kids in a negative example. They are not your tools or props to preach a sermon. They are your family. It is hard enough on them to be "on" every day as a pastor's spouse or preacher's kid. For their sakes, do not use examples that would reflect poorly on them. Don't worry. We know that they are far from perfect. After all, our kids play with your kids. Our spouses go to Bible study with your spouse. We've seen that occasional sourness between you and your beloved flesh of your flesh. After a few years of your pastorate, we've seen enough to know that your family has a long trip to get to heaven, perhaps even longer than ours. But we'd rather not hear it from the pulpit. I never worried a Sunday of my life about whether my father would trot out an embarrassing story from our home. If he mentioned my name, it was always with fondness and respect.

You, on the other hand, are open season. Illustrations about how miserably you have failed as a spouse, parent, pastor, and general human are happily accepted. But even here, have some restraint and consider the weaker brother and sister. Like anything, don't overdo it by emphasizing what a lout you are. Provide some balance. The Christian life is defined by its triumph over sin and temptation, the excitement of regeneration, of victories small and large, and the successful work of the Holy Spirit in sanctifying us. Christians should experience beauty more deeply than others, should hear songs with a richness that escapes those who don't commune with the Creator, and should find deeper satisfaction in the taste of food provided by our heavenly Father. Examples from your life of God "doing his thing," whether smooth or rough, can give great encouragement. For every three screw-ups, however, give us one of your "wins" as well.

Slice of Pizza or Sine Curve: Either Way, They'll Listen

Does your sermon have a "shape"? A great sermon goes somewhere and brings the congregation along for the ride. Of course, the best destination is the foot of God's throne. What if you got there? I imagine you'd feel somewhat thrilled. Enthusiastic? Scared? Full of awe and wonderment? Comforted? So shouldn't the congregation feel that way too when you deposit us there?

Sure thing, but how to do it?

Make sure that your sermon builds to that point of climax. If you are preaching Psalm 23, then your climax has been handed to you. It is feasting at the table of God forever. If you are preaching about the storm on the Sea of Galilee, the climax is Jesus reaching out to pull a drowning Peter to safety, alighting in the boat, and calming the storm. If you are preaching from Job about suffering, after all the extraordinary challenges he faces, the climax of the sermon is: "Before I had *heard* of you, now I have *seen* you." If you are preaching on Jesus in the garden after the resurrection, the climax of the sermon is his one word, "Mary."

Whatever you do, don't get to the climax before you have built the anticipation. Don't introduce the sermon of the resurrection by saying, "We see Mary in the garden wondering where Jesus has gone, and she doesn't even recognize him until he says to her 'Mary.' We're going to be talking about that today. It was a really neat and unexpected moment for her." A bit of a stomp on that punchline. Now where are you going to go?

Instead, build to the climax. The metaphor of "build" means establishing the foundation, raising the walls, installing the windows until it is tight to weather, carefully cutting and nailing the trim conditions, and so on. Spend the time setting out the fundamental factual and theological truths necessary to make that climax worth the wait.

Don't do it because we're playing some parlor game here. No, instead recognize that God wrote his book that way. He is the one who puts his people through challenges before demonstrating his power, his salvation, his way out, his grace, his love, and his skin-close presence. Name one brother or sister from the Bible who gets more than a mention, and I'll show you someone who went through something tough before they got the brass ring: Adam, Noah, Abraham, Jacob, Joseph, Moses, Joshua, Caleb, Hannah, Mordecai,

Esther, Samson, Ruth, Naomi, Hosea, Elijah, Deborah, Elisha, David, Solomon, Peter, Mary Magdalene, Saul/Paul, or Stephen. The punchlines of their lives would not have made any sense to them or us if God had disclosed them before the time was ripe.

In your preaching, go and do likewise. Set up the problem, explore its contours, plumb its depths, and only then solve it. Establish the tension of the drama, and only then resolve it. Pose the nagging question, show why it nags and even why it is a question, answer it the wrong way seven times, and then and only then give us the right and true answer.

Even your reading of the biblical passage will be important to building that tension and ultimate release. My sister, Gwenfair Adams, a professor of church history at Gordon-Conwell Theological Seminary, was once asked to read Scripture at a convocation at which the school's leading preacher was to preach. She studied the text the week prior to the event and saw that there were several ways to read it that would elicit different emphases. So she called her colleague. Sure enough, when she queried whether she should read it one way or another, the preacher exclaimed "Thanks for calling!" and confirmed that she should not emphasize one particular aspect lest she ruin the peak of his sermon.

As you prepare your sermon, chart its shape. Where is the high point? As you preach it, know that you are building toward that moment. When you arrive there, allow the power of that peak to move your congregation. Don't step on the moment. Then, in the time immediately following that moment is when you will be best able to promise sweet grace, offer encouragement, challenge for change, or set out a goal. And because you shaped your sermon, your intention will have the best chance of being realized.

Extemporaneous Ain't What You Think It Is

I was at a banquet celebrating a church's fiftieth anniversary. Among the attendees were many of the current members of the church, past members who had moved away, former staff and pastors, and the odd assortment of dignitaries and representatives from other churches and community groups. Although there was a set schedule of events and speakers, as the master of ceremonies recognized various persons of importance, he departed from that order at one point and called on one of the prior pastors to come forward.

What happened next was inspiring to anyone who enjoys a display of fine public speaking. The former pastor took the microphone and began to extemporize. He spoke about some favorite stories from his tenure at the church. His various gentle caricatures of beloved long-time members had us all damaging our innards laughing so hard. By the end, we were reminded why we had liked him so much. He walked back to his table to the warmest applause of the evening.

Most remarkable to us was the fact that he had not been asked to speak beforehand. He was not listed on the program. He just went "off the cuff."

Many times, the response of people witnessing such extemporizing is to say, "That guy's amazing; he just did that all off the top of his head! How does he do that with no preparation?" Which then leads inevitably to the negative comparison, "I could never do that."

What we often fail to recognize is that this "extemporaneous" speech, that impromptu result of "bring us a word, Pastor," is often the product of tremendous preparation. Three kinds of preparation, in fact.

Preparation Type 1. There is simply the preparation that a life at the pulpit or podium provides. The more you preach and the more you speak to an audience, the deeper the reservoir of experiences upon which to draw.

Drew Carey, the comic, hosted a show based on impromptu comedy called *Whose Line Is It Anyway*? Each show consisted of sketches and songs all performed "spur of the moment." For example, Carey might ask the audience to tell him two professions. "Neurosurgeon" and "jockey," the crowd might shout out. Or maybe "actuary." Or "butcher." Or "website designer." Carey would then set a scene: "An actuary and neurosurgeon are climbing Kilimanjaro when a storm comes in." Off the actors would go, creating a usually hilarious interaction between these two. All "unrehearsed." The draw of the show and the reason we all enjoy impromptu is the how-in-the-world-ness of it.

I got a better glimpse of how during my senior year at college. A close friend of mine, who was in one of the campus impromptu theater groups, invited me to attend one of their performances. This group would hold shows from time to time, and the drama, story, plot, and resulting presentation were created at the moment, tabula rasa, right there in front of us.

Or were they?

I happened to know that in the six weeks leading up to the performance, my friend had been out five to six nights a week, practicing three to four hours a night with the other members of the troupe. They would try out all kinds of situational comic or even tragic settings. They pushed the boundaries together of their creativity, wit, pathos, and overall acting abilities. All of them together practicing exhaustively for their "impromptu" theater performance.

Few of us have the true ad lib glib genius of Jonathan Winters or Robin Williams. But if we shrug off that deficiency and spend a little time anticipating the unrehearsed moments, we may handle them with greater aplomb.

Preparation Type 2. The other preparation is specific for this group, tonight. We must acknowledge the reality that you the preacher, a public figure, must be ready at any time to speak. You simply do not know when you will be called out of your comfortable seat tucked in the back of the hall to address the group.

It may simply be a request to open in prayer or give a benediction. Or it may be "a word" or remarks. Whatever it is, you can be ready if you spend a few minutes beforehand prognosticating.

We have a Thanksgiving Day "fun run" in Ipswich, the town where my church is located. For a few years in a row, the organizers have asked our senior pastor to offer a word of prayer. One year, however, he was ill and unable to attend. As the runners lined up, the organizer spotted our associate pastor and asked him to pray. Now you might say, "Pastors pray all the time, so what's the big deal?" But don't forget that this is the northeast region of our fair country where Christ's name is uttered publicly only when someone bangs their shin into a cement mixer. Without as much as the nine seconds it took him to work through the crowd of runners and grab the mic, our associate fashioned a fine prayer weaving in the Thanksgiving theme along with the beauty of countryside and the thrill of physical endeavor, all while being God-centered. All spur of the moment.

Or had he anticipated the senior pastor's absence and guessed . . . ?

How can we prepare? Even running through a few questions as you drive to the event may help you be ready. What's the point of the evening? In what capacity are you attending? Who will be there? What's the overall program? If you were asked to participate, in what role would it be? You can probably run through those before you've finished buckling your seatbelt.

Preparation Type 3. The final bit is to do a Nehemiah. As we know, Nehemiah was the taster for King Artaxerxes during the exile of Israel. He had just heard from his countrymen visiting from Judah that Jerusalem lay in ruins. As he went in to the king to serve him wine, the king queried why he looked so sad. Nehemiah was suddenly fearful, perhaps in part because if you are the king's wine taster, looking unhappy or ill is not a recipe for long-term success. When he gave the king the briefest overview of the cause of his gloominess, Artaxerxes then asked him what he wanted.

Before answering, Nehemiah "prayed to the God of heaven." He then gave his response.

Whatever your preparation, whatever your emotional state at the moment, however sure or unsure you are of what you are about to say, remember that you always speak as God's ambassador. Ask him for help. You may not have more time than "Help!" but he knows well what you need and he will provide it.

Don't Go Back-to-Back with the Same Emotion

If you try for sadness once, you'll get it. Try again, and the congregation's emotional experience is weakened by 50 percent. Try a third time, and you'll actually get the *opposite* emotional reaction. For example, three tries in a row at sadness will elicit nervous giggles and chuckles. Three tries in a row at humor will fall flat and sour and even perhaps annoy the hearers. Three tries in a row at an emotion of sweetness will actually elicit a response of cynicism or sarcasm.

My father was a master at applying this principle. He would push the congregation to the brink of despair over their sinfulness. His face would be almost angry, his voice raised and powerful. And just when we felt we couldn't take it anymore, he would pull back, a smile would come to his face, and he would speak a word of grace, of comfort. His hand would turn palm upward. His countenance would change. And with it, we would be drawn back from despair or fear to the hope of the gospel.

Radio Audiences

If your sermon will be broadcast on the radio, the occasional reference to your radio listeners is appropriate and helpful. If you are using a visual aid, you may want to describe it a bit "for the folks at home." It keeps your congregation praying for those who are listening. It draws in those who are listening via radio to make them feel included.

Too much acknowledgment of the silent, invisible audience, however, and it will seem contrived. I remember being present for a sermon from one preacher who was also on TV. He spent most of the sermon looking at the camera rather than his congregation. Great for those watching on TV. Terrible for the rest of us. I felt a distinct lack of connection. Instead of being the flock he wanted to feed that morning, we were his studio audience with all but an applause sign lighting up at appropriate times. I half expected us to "go to commercial break" in the middle of his sermon.

When to Start Your Sermon Prep

You have just been asked to preach a sermon series at a retreat six months from now for a church four states away. The phone call interrupted you as you were weeding the marigolds on a Saturday. Assuming that you think you should accept the invitation, when should you begin to prepare?

Now. Just after you hang up the phone.

Pray that God gives you the appropriate message, even if your hosts have already told you your subject matter. Begin jotting down what you know about the church, the state, the denomination, the makeup of the group that will be attending, your connection to the group, the person with whom you will be working to coordinate your visit, the time of year for the retreat, the location of the retreat, the number and kinds of people who normally attend, whether it's coed or not, and so on.

Ask for a few church bulletins, the monthly newsletter, the titles and texts of the past three retreats. Ask your contact what kinds of issues the church has been dealing with in the past year. Any exciting new ministry ventures? Any challenges? Tragedies? Any abiding sin patterns? Any major specific spiritual needs?

Nail down the details. What is the schedule for the retreat? When will you be speaking? How many times? For how long? What does the venue look like? What comes immediately before you speak? What comes immediately after? What goals does the leadership have for the retreat? Why have they chosen you for this year's event? Assume nothing; confirm everything.

Let's consider the typical church men's retreat, where you'll be handed the topic, "Being a Warrior for Jesus." We know that the men will arrive for dinner after a two-hour drive from work on a Friday evening. They will have games after your first session and then go to bed. You will have two more sessions, one in the morning after breakfast and one in the late afternoon following five hours of outdoor manly recreation.

Given that information, you should immediately see that the tone of the three modules will need to be strikingly different.

Friday night will find the men tired after a full day, a long drive, and a big dinner (hanger steaks and baked potatoes, let's say). They will be trying to decompress from their week's work. They will be zonked and ready for bed.

Saturday morning will find them fired up, pen and pad of paper in hand, glad to be away from the demands of home life and beneficially disconnected from their customary duties and worries. Some will be blurry-eyed from a late night game of "Risk" or "Monopoly." But they'll be ready for a challenge.

Saturday evening will find them happily exhausted from Ultimate Frisbee, Foosball, soccer, swimming, boating, and hiking. But they'll also have their cars packed and be ready to go home to see their wives and kids, reenter their day-to-day schedules, and begin making inspired changes to their lives.

Those three contexts each demand a different approach. Friday Night: Ease into the talk, tell some jokes, connect with the men, help them transition and lay out the essential theme of the weekend with an initial treatment of the subject, nothing crazy heavy. Saturday morning: Get into it deep, go after them with real challenges, make them think about their lives and their need to get serious about whatever God is telling them. Saturday evening: No new ground here; just overview what you've discussed through the weekend with some practical action points.

You can see that finding out the schedule for the retreat after you've arrived on Friday afternoon is not going to give you a whole lot of time to reconfigure your presentations. So get that information early and dovetail your preparation appropriately.

If Applications Are the Frosting on the Cake, Remember That the Fork Hits That Layer First

As a kid, I really liked the cake's frosting the most. To maximize the pleasure, I would eat around the frosting, starting with the bottom of the cake with all its dryness, working my way up the layers until all that was left was the frosting. All that wonderful creamy sweetness on my fork with nary a crumb of cake to bother it.

But, of course, with time I began to realize that the frosting and the layers and the cake were all meant to collaborate, creating a wonderfully rich gastronomic experience free from either chalky cakiness or sickly saccharinity. I saw that the part I had been saving until last was always the first thing my fork hit on the way to the bottom.

The average preacher will approach their sermon the way I did my cake as a seven-year-old, as if the applications are the frosting. They'll wrap up their sermon with a first and final nod to some sort application—25.6 minutes will have gone by. We'll have heard the Scripture read. We'll have been enlightened about the historical background. We'll have heard some quotes from some theologians. We'll have listened carefully to some cross-references. We'll have a pretty good sense of what the main passage is about. On good days, there may even have been some lively illustrations.

Then, as we sense that the sermon is winding down (primarily because we notice the organist slipping back onto her bench and the ushers surreptitiously sliding the offering plates from under the back pew), the pastor spreads on a quick application—essentially, an "Oh, by the way, try doing this next week" parting shot.

But what a missed opportunity. If the Scriptures are intended to have an effect on us, then tell us what that is supposed to be throughout the sermon. If your sermon has four points, you should suggest how each of those points matters to us. How will that point you just made change me, my life, and my circumstances? What am I supposed to do with that fact, principle, or nugget you just painstakingly explained to me?

Here's the crux: Answer those questions before you leave one point to move on to the next. Let your sermonic fork slice through the icing, fudge, ganache, cake, and other fillings, and even pick up a dollop of whipped cream with each forkful.

Why in the World Did He Choose That Text?

By the time my father graduated from seminary, he had preached over seven hundred times. All across Wales there were always plenty of pulpits that relied on circuit preachers and student preachers. So my father could preach twice on a Sunday and get back to his studies on Monday. But in our family lore, it was his first sermon that was the most famous of all seven hundred.

It was the tradition that any student going off to university to study to become a pastor would preach the first sermon of his nascent career in his home pulpit. At seventeen, my father mounted the pulpit at the Rose of Sharon chapel in Llanelli, Wales, to stand before four hundred fifty expectant congregants. In later years, he would often recount how he preached on the second coming of Christ. When he strode to the door to greet the worshippers for the first time as the morning's preacher, many were polite and some were more vocal. Several patronizingly assured him that after he had had "some learning" at the university, he would come to understand that the second coming was metaphorical and not the factual reality he had just preached.

Fifty years later, he would often tell us that only one person out of the four hundred and fifty—namely, his father—agreed with his interpretation that Jesus was actually coming back.

For some strange reason, my sister and I never bothered to ask him the obvious questions: Why in the world had he chosen a text that resulted in such a negative response? Why not choose 1 Corinthians 13 on love, or something as innocuous? Unfortunately, my father took that information to his grave. Or so we thought.

In 2003, we hosted a gentleman from Wales, a pastor-scholar who was in the United States to present a seminar on the 1904 revival in Wales. It turned out that he was one of the world's experts on the topic and had been preparing to lead centennial celebrations throughout Wales and beyond.

At dinner, the talk turned to the effect of the revival on Wales. I remembered my father's first sermon and queried of our guest how could it be that in 1939, only one generation after the 1904 Revival, so many people had strayed in their thinking so that they now held that the second coming was metaphorical and not actual? And why in the world did my father preach on such a controversial text?

To the day I die, I will never forget the explosive excitement this fellow exuded as he provided the historical context for what had been a family mystery. He set out that my father would have undoubtedly belonged to the movement of youthful Christians in Wales who were the next generation beneficiaries of the revival. They would have been in their late teens to early twenties. They were trying to take back the church and were arguing for the historicity of the Gospels and the necessity of the work of Christ in the lives of believers. The second coming was one of their Shibboleth texts. This scholar likened my seventeen-year-old father to John Wayne walking up to the pulpit with his guns strapped to his side, ready for a showdown!

That evening after dinner, I called my sister to tell her that we had a guest unlocking family mysteries by explaining things about our father from sixty-five years ago. I encouraged her to come for breakfast the next day to hear it herself. She arrived at 7:30 a.m. Within two and a half minutes, the bachelor pastor-scholar had fallen in love with her. Four minutes later, my equally single sister reciprocated. They wed the following year.

Maybe that's why God had my father preach that sermon on Christ's second coming.

What's Your Sermon's Elevator Speech?

The elevator speech is firmly ensconced in the lore of business-speak. You're a young middle manager in a Fortune 500 company. One morning, you get on the elevator to go to the fortieth floor to deliver a document to the executive assistant of the CEO. By happenstance, the CEO joins you on that trip. Just the two of you in that elevator. What will you say during that thirty-four-second trip to the penthouse that will impress this CEO and launch your executive career? What can you say about yourself that will be memorable and will differentiate you from the other two hundred fifty middle managers? If you are smart, you will have that speech prepared and ready for prime time. It will be streamlined and laser-like in its impact.

If your sermon got on that elevator, what would it say? Can you describe this coming Sunday's message with a thirty-four-second level of precision and focus? If you cannot, then you are not ready for your sermon.

From a Patristic to Scooby-Doo

From its inception fifty years ago, my home church has drawn heavily from the students, faculty, and staff of Gordon College and Gordon-Conwell Theological Seminary. Many of the students working on their master of divinity degrees have volunteered for our ministries and brought great energy and vitality to the church. With some of those planning to enter pastoral ministry, we have tried to give them the opportunity to preach by scheduling them at our evening service. That particular service is attended by about 4 percent of the congregation. These twenty to thirty stalwart faithful are often subjected to what can be best described as "works in progress," as those sermons are often the first "live" ones the students have ever preached.

Then one day, there was a bit of a buzz. Apparently, in the prior Sunday's evening service, one of these seminarians had delivered a memorable sermon. It so happened that we were between pastors and patch-quilting together Sunday morning preachers.

Based on the buzz, for the first time in the church's history, the board of elders invited a student to preach at the morning services. And preach he did. He opened up the Scriptures in deeply satisfying ways. He challenged us. In one sermon, he called on the entire church to pray Paul's prayer in Ephesians 3:14–19 *every day until Easter.* At twenty-five years old, he preached like he had forty years of ministry under his belt. In the years since, I have continued to hear about people who did indeed pray that prayer every day until Easter, and beyond. His sermons evidenced the fact that for years he had been reading through the entire Bible *every three months.*

Part of his giftedness lay in being able to illustrate in the freshest of ways. In one sermon, he drew on illustrations from the first-century Patristics all the way to the twentieth-century cartoon character Scooby-Doo. We all listened attentively because we had no idea what was coming next, but we knew it would be good. Nobody left bored. Everyone left understanding God and his word a bit better and deeper. There was something in those sermons for every person in the pew.

Dealing with Distractions in the Pulpit

There are two kinds of distractions: yours and ours. Eliminate yours and address ours.

What are your distractions? Those distractions are things you do that detract from your ability to communicate your sermon. We start focusing on those things rather than your words.

Perhaps you are always concerned about the time, so you keep looking at your watch. I've seen some preachers take off their leather-strapped watch and with some emphasis place it carefully on the pulpit. And then forget about it entirely. Do like many churches and stick a clock on the back wall where you can glance at it without drawing attention to the fact.

Or perhaps you have some physical voluntary "tic" that has crept into your preaching style. For example, from time to time during your sermon, you adjust your tie, rub your forehead, move your glasses up your nose until they slip down again, hitch up your trousers, or tap your left foot against the base of the pulpit. Whatever it is, take the necessary action or start practicing to stop doing it. Before the service, ask your spouse how you look, and then forget about it. If you rub your forehead, make sure that it fits what you are saying or somehow otherwise communicates something beneficial. Go back to the ophthalmologist and get your glasses tightened. Buy suspenders or lose weight. Quit tapping your left foot against the base of the pulpit.

Then there are our distractions. A fire truck blares its sirens as it passes the church. A jet plane thunders overhead. A child begins screaming and the mother will not remove her. Someone in the congregation drops his huge Ryrie Study Bible on the floor. The wind howls through the trees outside. A homeless man suffering from dementia stumbles in the back door. A couple of neighbors start a Sunday morning kerfuffle down the street.

In one service I attended, the pastor was holding forth on a very wide platform. A man, for no apparent reason, walked slowly across the entire platform *behind* the pastor, all the way to the other side. When he got there, he stood in front of a plant, did nothing to the plant, and then slowly ambled back across, again behind the pastor, opened the door and went out.

You probably want to know why he did that. Sorry, neither I nor anyone else there figured it out. Worse, the preacher did not become aware of the drama until later at Sunday dinner.

Assuming, however, that you experience the event along with the congregation, what can you do about these psychological impositions?

Ignore. Sometimes it is best simply to ignore. Things such as sneezes, a coughing jag, or other noisome bodily function, someone abruptly departing from the front row, or a door slamming in the distance can be ignored without much problem. People are able to filter them out and politeness compels you to avoid embarrassing a particular person.

Acknowledge. Some distractions simply can't be ignored and can't be incorporated. If a jet flies directly overhead while you are exhorting people to live God-filled marriages, start singing "I'm leavin' on a jet plane, don't know when I'll be back again." Perhaps that is a bit of a stretch, but it beats losing to the airplane. But sometimes you just have to wait until the jet passes, look out the window with a quizzical grin and chuckle to the congregation without doing more. It will relax your hearers and allow you all to get back to the meat of your sermon.

Incorporate. This is the most challenging of the possible responses. It requires some quick thinking if the event is a sudden one. Sometimes those events seem to be provided by God as some sort of percussion. In the middle of a section about God's judgment, thunder rolls or the lights dim? Too rich. On the other hand, some sounds are chronic, such as the rumble of a rooftop air-conditioning unit or a bulldozer working next door. You have more time to incorporate them. Make those distractions work for you.

Stop preaching. I know of one couple who visited a large denominational church, and—while hundreds listened and the preacher did his thing—a man had a heart attack about fifteen pews from the front. The stalwart preacher preached on. The ushers called for an ambulance. The sermon continued. The paramedics wheeled a stretcher all the way down the center aisle, lifted the man onto it, and then wheeled him out. Not a break in sermonic stride did our preacher make.

The visiting couple never went back.

PowerPoint

I suppose I am first compelled to opine on the propriety of using PowerPoint while preaching. Even raising the question sounds peskily neo-Luddite. The Luddites' descendants will, with great urgency, state that we must not allow technology to encroach upon our worship. Doing so will fundamentally change our experience of God in worship. Fair enough. Others will counterpoint equally emphatically that all technology is to be used to present the gospel and to edify the believer. Failing to do so merely abdicates beneficial tools to Satan. Fair enough again.

The debate is always worth having whenever new technologies appear. I chaired a church strategic planning team where we actually spent some time exploring the boundaries of the "virtual pastor." Was it important that our pastor be able to preach, or could we bring in a person with strong small group ministry and other skills, and then simply rent videos of established great preachers? Of course, our discussion was a bit tongue in cheek, but the intent was real. We were pushing the limits to see both what we felt about the merit and importance of sitting under real, live preaching and the appropriateness of using certain technologies in the worship service.

Fifteen years later, when faced with a space crunch for our Sunday morning worship services, I and my fellow elders debated the possibility of running two simultaneous worship services in two different buildings on our campus with a video feed of our pastor into one of the services while he preached "live and in person" in the other. It is an approach that is now foundational to most multisite churches.

After vigorous discussion, we decided that the pastor's physical presence was too high a value, and we just ran our preachers ragged by requiring them to preach back to back in the same hour in two of our three services. I know of at least one church with two campuses and eleven thousand members where the preacher flies by helicopter between services. Now that's commitment to being there in person.

But back to PowerPoint.

The key to effective PowerPoint is seamlessness. Do all that you can to keep the technology from distracting the congregation. If you can outsource the button, do so. My brother-in-law, Kevin, is one of the best at using PowerPoint in the pulpit. He made an early decision never to be the guy who punches the computer's up or down arrow to "go – to – the – next – slide." Instead, he provides a fairly detailed outline including notations on each slide to his tech person. Then he just preaches. The techie keeps the slides rolling, smoothly matching Kevin as he moves from point to point, text to text, and illustration to illustration. If Kevin goes "off script," the techie goes to a dark screen until Kevin returns.

Key to all this seamlessness is the fact that Kevin never looks at the screen. If you ever watch a group of birders toting binoculars and chasing a warbler through a forest, forget about the bird and watch the birders. Warblers are tiny little birds that flit and dart and dip with a predilection to spending their feeding times up high in the trees. There's an actual syndrome called Warbler Neck for the pain and soreness some birders end up experiencing as they try to keep the possessed bird within their field of vision.

If you continually look up at the monitor behind you for your very own PowerPoint presentation, you will suffer from PowerPoint Neck. But even worse, if we follow you every time you follow your own PowerPoint and we follow the PowerPoint and we follow you during the times you are not following your own PowerPoint, we'll end up developing our own ailment, PowerPoint Eyeballs.

As to the content, forgive me stating the obvious, but be careful that the technology helps and does not hinder. Bible texts, of course, can assist the congregation and lessen the time they spend and the breeze they create hunting through their Bibles. ("Some" would say that that substituting an overhead version is not a good thing and contributes to our biblical illiteracy.)

Pictures can replace those thousand words that you would otherwise have spent trying to describe the very thing that now presents itself in digital format on your 8'x10' screen. ("Some" would say that that just capitulates to the lowest common denominator and may engender laziness in preaching.) Video clips may contextualize the truths you are presenting. ("Some" would say that this flies the white flag in admitting that preaching is not as exciting as the latest blockbuster film or popular show.)

What's my opinion? I'm a tiny bit "Some." But I'll probably go soft on that in the coming years. Like much else done in the pulpit, when done well, it can be superb.

What's the "Elephant in the Corner"? (Part 3)

When I chaired our church's senior pastoral search committee, we spent a good deal of time trying to figure out how to evaluate the preaching of the various candidates. There are a few well-known principles that most search committees follow in requesting sermon tapes. For instance, one such guidepost is to request three *consecutive* Sunday sermons. Most preachers develop a sermon or two that they think is their "best." They spend a great deal of time on it; perhaps even include a few extra illustrations and applications. They preach it in several churches to smooth out the kinks, and then they send you the tape of their best version. That, of course, is not the preacher you'll be getting. We want to know what they are like Sunday after Sunday.

One of our pastoral searches happened to stretch into 2002. So we came up with a rather unique litmus test and requested a fourth sermon: the one each candidate preached on September 16, 2001. That sermon told us more about the preacher's pastoral heart and ability to apply Scripture to one of the most unimaginable and horrific days in United States history than any other investigative technique could have. How did those candidates treat that event in the life of their church? What texts did they use? If I were on another search committee in twenty years, I'd still ask for that sermon! The man we eventually called preached one of the best sermons on the events of September 11 that we heard, handling it with wisdom and sensitivity.

On the other hand, our visiting preacher on September 16 preached on Isaiah 9 or 10 (but not the nice bits about a child being born). I'm vague because so many years later I'm still stunned. Go ahead and read it. You will quickly notice phrases such as "bricks have fallen down," "wickedness burns like a fire," "land will be scorched," and "people will be fuel for the fire."

Now add this fact to the mix. *He never mentioned what had happened in New York City just five days earlier.* For reasons unknown, he had decided weeks prior to preach that sermon to us on his one visit into town. Beyond any comprehension, it never occurred to him that he might have wanted to address the events of September 11.

If you were in church on September 16, 2001, you will remember being joined by thousands of people who had not entered a church in decades. We had our share. One woman had finally come to church for the first time after years of gentle coaxing by one of our members. The week's events had laid bare in her soul a deep need for comfort and answers. It pains me to my core to tell you that after hearing the sermon, she vowed she would never return. As far as I know, she has kept true to her pledge.

The gospel is relevant. Christ is present in today's world. He came down to the miasma of our lives. He has our dirt on his hands, a deep permanent scar in his side from our spear thrust, marred hands and feet, all because of our filth.

Sometimes we have seen the elephant and the elephant is us. Sometimes it's an event that horrifically spotlights how terrible we humans are.

How can the church's preaching ever be anything but fully connected and even entwined with the day-to-day realities of this world?

X Chromosomes (Part 1)

Aside from the actual reading of Scripture, take liberal care often to replace "him" with "her," "his" with "hers," "he" with "she," and so on. If you are preaching to the average congregation, you probably have more women than men. If you are the average male preacher, however, you probably use many more masculine pronouns than feminine, many more manly illustrations than womanly, refer to many more male names, male hobbies, male historical figures, male biblical persons, male colors, male approaches, male endeavors, male accomplishments, male smells, male clothes, male, male, male. Illustrations generally get mined from the sports world, field of battle, political history, cars, derring-do, action movies, power tools, and fatherhood.

It is absolutely necessary to draw upon things that will reach and relate to the women listening to you each week. Where possible, simply use the feminine pronoun. If an illustration could just as easily feature a woman, do so. "A salesman asks the boy if his dog bites. The boy says no. The salesman pets the dog and the dog bites him. He exclaims: 'I thought you said your dog doesn't bite.' The boy replies, 'He doesn't. That isn't my dog.'" Retell it with a girl instead of a boy as the primary actor. You haven't lost anything. Instead, you've casually included all the women.

It's a bit more effort for some guys to find illustrations that are female in orientation. But this is where you become a true and full man. Talk to the women in your life. Your wife and her friends can be a rich source of knowledge. What activities excite them? What news stories catch their eyes? What's "in" in their lives? How about your daughter and her friends? What's in her backpack? What is she spending her allowance on? What bothers her? Why is she laughing? Crying? What about the women who work with you at the church? What are they talking about these days? What are their interests? When you walk into a committee meeting and folks are chatting up the day, what are the women discussing? Join in. Listen. Ask questions. What are the vignettes that capture their essential experiences?

You should be doing all these things anyway as a part of your ministry. But there's the added imperative of enriching your preaching with the knowledge that you glean from the women in your life.

This interest in women should be a touchstone of your life and ministry. After putting down this chapter, you may luck out and get an illustration for this week's sermon from a conversation this week. But it is more likely that as you develop a profound understanding of the hopes, challenges, fears, dreams, experiences, and lives of the women of your congregation and within your sphere, the resulting empathy and knowledge will infuse your preaching. You will use those examples because they come naturally and flow like all the other manly ones.

Y Chromosomes

If you are a woman, reverse the above. Remember that almost half the congregation grew up giving noogies to their siblings, playing with insects, eating dirt, glorifying Wilt Chamberlain, Dr. J., Larry Bird, Michael Jordan, or LeBron James, and generally doing Y-chromosome type things. Make sure you include illustrations that reach their experiences.

There has been a rash of books written recently about the manliness of Christian men. We are warriors. We want challenges. We fight for truth, honor, women, and country. We do stupid things as long as they give us glory. We risk the absurd just to prove the potency of our testosterone.

Infuse your preaching with connections to your marvelous males.

Who's This Oprah Person You're Talking About?

A word or two about the necessity of cultural literacy. There's something mildly peculiar about a pastor who knows the details of the current plotlines from *Days of Our Lives*. But there's something that's just out of touch about a pastor in America who has no idea what *Days of Our Lives* refers to. (The soap opera, okay? Stay with me here.)

Jesus knew what was going on around him in his culture, government, politics, towns, religious hierarchies, and human interactions. Paul drew on his knowledge of the persecution of Christians, and there's also no doubt he was deeply knowledgeable concerning the temptations common to his fellow Christians. You'll be in safe company if you pay attention to those things.

Why not subscribe to and read a local paper and city paper and perhaps a basic weekly magazine such as *Time* or *The Week*? Go ahead and watch the news once in a while. Do some channel surfing from time to time. I am not suggesting that you should get bogged down in Hollywood's worst offerings. Remember, even angels avoid looking into evil things. But have some idea what your congregation is watching. And know that the people you and your congregation are trying to reach for the gospel are extremely literate in these things.

At any given time, you should have at least a passing acquaintance with your culture. What are the current crazes? What's "in"? What's "out"? Who's "hot"? Who's "not"? What's big-time in your locale? The high school football team? Sit in the local coffee shop and maybe become a "regular."

What's the payoff for your preaching? You will understand your audience. You will become attuned to the temptations facing your congregation and be better able to fortify your flock. You will find treasure troves of illustrations and applications for your sermons. Your sermons will gain an immediacy, a freshness, and an urgency. You'll be a better preacher.

If It's Good Enough for the Grateful Dead, It Should Be Good Enough for You

"Hey Walters, wait just a minute. Are you suggesting that my sermons, based on the eternal truths of Scripture, have no staying power and just disappear like the mist on a summer's morning burned by the heat of the sun?"

Not really. But, as I state in other ways in several other of these chapters, when you preach, preach to the people sitting before you and listening right then. When you are preparing your sermon, pray that the Holy Spirit will quicken within you sensitivities to the scriptural text so as to emphasize what this particular group of people needs to hear. Pick illustrations that will reach this specific congregation, on this specific Sunday. Use words that will make sense to this body of listeners.

One of my roommates in college was a Deadhead. A Deadhead is a devotee of the boundary-bending fusion rock band called the Grateful Dead. He, as so many of those Deadheads have done, has gone on to become a professional and fine contributor to society—in this case, as an attorney, husband, and father. But during those college years, he would do his best to attend the Dead's somewhat psychedelic concerts whenever they came within a few hundred miles of our dorm room. He was even kind enough to bring back bootleg recordings and lull us both to sleep at three or four in the morning after the concert. (One of the two of us, oddly enough, having already been asleep for five or six hours before then.)

Any devotee of the Dead will tell you that the genius of the band lay in the fact that no two performances of any song in their repertoire were identical. Certainly, at its core the song would be the same with the same melody, the same overall chord structure and the same lyrics. But in any specific performance, the different bandmates would take turns featuring their instruments, playing around the melodies, creating new harmonies, new rhythms, and new tempos each time they played a song. The result was that any fan could attend two concerts on two consecutive nights and never hear the same song twice, even if the playlists were identical.

Your sermons should be at least as good as a Dead song. If only for the sake of the organist who has to listen to you twice or three times on a Sunday morning, mix it up a bit. To reach the congregation before you, swap out illustrations, change your phrasing, use different words, and emphasize different parts of the content. It will force you away from preaching as an act and toward preaching as communication.

The "Head" Voice

Have you thought much about how your voice sounds to your congregation? Remember, we sit there, week after week, listening to you speak for half an hour or more.

Experiment a bit with making your voice sound different. I don't mean try to do a Jerry Seinfeld cartoon voiceover. But see how your voice can be moderated by the way you produce the sound and use air.

Test 1: Produce the voice from up behind your nose, essentially from your eyeball sockets. See how that sounds? If you are doing it correctly, you will sound at least a bit nasally.

Test 2: Now start moving the voice down all the way to the back of your throat and even down to your stomach. It should sound strained and hard.

Test 3: Exhale as much air as you possibly can and try Tests 1 and 2.

Test 4: Inhale as much air as you possibly can and try Tests 1 and 2.

Test 5: Now try both Tests 1 and 2 at the same time and produce your voice with reasonably full diaphragm so that it comes straight from the back of your throat. The sound should include a bit of your nose, but without being nasally. Some suggest feeling the voice go right out the top of your head.

That's your "head voice." You should be able to use your head voice for much longer without straining. The volume should be better as well. Most of all, the sound should be smoother and therefore easier to listen to. Give it a try this Sunday.

References to "Those Kinds" of Movies and Books

When is it appropriate to refer to a movie with an R rating for violence or sexuality or "adult themes," or to a book that used to be on a banned list? Sure, *Deliverance* or *Lady Chatterley's Lover* may provide a perfect illustration, but will it edify your congregation to know the details? Or, perhaps more subtly, to know that you watched the film or read the book?

Take great care here. I have seen borderline movies appropriately put to service as an illustration but almost always with some caveat: "I don't recommend this movie to watch, but I refer to it this morning as a powerful illustration of . . ." Or even better: "I've not seen this movie/read this book but am familiar with the *Great Literature for Dummies* version. In it, Lady Chatterley finds herself in a loveless marriage . . ."

A little secret: I've neither seen *Deliverance* nor read *Lady Chatterley's Lover*, but I was nonetheless able to refer to them in what I trust was a helpfully illustrative manner for my point.

You Know Greatness When You See It

College students are some of the most intellectually fired up inhabitants of this planet. Their brains are being stretched daily. They are learning things that nobody else has ever known. They have come to the well-founded conclusion for the first time that people of greater than twenty-two years of age have no idea about much of anything. They have often shed the naive faith of their parents, trading it for the wisdom of dead people with German or French names. And they are ripe for the picking.

As a member of the Harvard Radcliffe Christian Fellowship, I had a keen interest in evangelism. The group agreed to host a lecture for the Harvard campus to be given by Os Guinness. Dr. Guinness is an exceedingly brainy Brit with all the great attributes thereof. He graciously agreed to come and speak futuristically concerning the state of faith and religion in America.

The privilege fell to me to emcee the event, which was to consist of forty-five minutes of Dr. Guinness speaking followed by a question/answer time. We had rented Lecture Hall D in Harvard's Science Center, which is a banked room with theater seats. When we arrived, I discovered that the maintenance crew had locked up all the lecterns and stands. There was no microphone. No podium. Nada. Just a wide open naked space in front of all these rabid Harvardians. I was a little panicked.

Dr. Guinness, however, did not appear ruffled in the least. I queried where he would want to put his notes. He expressed no concern, and it soon became apparent why. After I introduced him to the crowd, he held forth for those forty-five minutes without a single piece of paper. Without a single verbal pause. And his hands spent no time in his pockets fiddling with his car keys. Making it all the more impressive, please note that this was no "What I Did for My Summer Vacation" speech. This was dense, carefully reasoned, and tightly argued apologetics and cultural analysis.

When he finished, I took the floor to moderate the Q&A. The first question out was from an arrogant Harvard student (some would say that's redundant). In true Cantabrigian fashion, it was more of a comment than a question. For his critique of Dr. Guinness's presentation, the student drew from some article I had never read and written by a person I had never heard of. I started sweating. The whole point of bringing this Os guy to Harvard was to show the non-Christian students, with all their supposed erudition, that Christianity was a religion with intellectual heft. Here we were, right out of the box, about to challenge that concept. Or so I thought.

Dr. Guinness listened carefully and graciously, thanked the student for his astute "question," and then proceeded to (a) outline the cited article's deficiencies, (b) explain why the writer was incorrect in his conclusions, (c) suggest that if the student were to read three pages further in that article, he would have found a countervailing thought, (d) suggest some other works by that author that the student had not yet read, and (e) elucidate why those other works were also faulty. Next question, please.

I take comfort in knowing that God made some Christians off-the-charts smart.

Applications of Gnarly Stuff

Even the most abstract theological concept can be applied. Indeed, it *must* be applied.

Why don't we flesh out an example? You've decided to preach through the attributes of God. You've come to God's self-sufficiency. God is God and has no need of anything or anyone else. He does not improve. He cannot be augmented, added to, or increased in any way. He is who he is. Period.

It's a truth that seems to scream of inapplicability. In fact, by its definition, it seems like thumbing the eye of humanity. It seems to eliminate any of our relevance and with it any relevance of the theological concept to our lives. If God can live well enough without us, doesn't that mean that he would be complete without us, and doesn't that fact set him so far apart from us so as to have no impact in our lives?

But let's ponder this anew. If God has no need of us, then he is completely self-contained. Therefore, he must be wealth defined. He has and is the riches of the universe. But because we are talking about it, it must mean that his self-containedness does not mean that he is incommunicative. He obviously has reached out of that state of self-sufficient being to create us and to commune with us.

We are, on the other hand, if nothing else, hopelessly needy. We need air. We need food. We need shelter. We need companionship. We need health. We need money. We need until the day we die. And then, boy, do we need!

But now, see where this is going. Because God made us, he must have made us out of his complete lack of need. He made me and you simply because he wanted to. And with that, as we know from Scripture, comes his self-imposed obligation to give from his infinite self-sufficiency all that we need. In him we live and move and have our being.

By now, you should see the applications looming on the horizon. All that theological truth propels us to this conclusion: We can trust God! Rat-a-tat come the applications: Tomorrow when I go to work to face those three colleagues who have my worst interests at heart, I can know that God will give me all that I need not only because he has promised it, but also because he can. As I return home today to my nonbelieving husband who will be angry because I went to church, I can show him love, because God is Love to me. As I face another week of crippling back pain, I can do all things through Christ, because he is and has everything and will give freely to me.

Apply that as you speak it.

As well, because he and nothing else is self-sufficient, he and nothing else is worthy of our worship. If we're looking for anything or anyone to get excited about this week, we can't do any better than getting excited about God.

Apply that as you speak it.

The very fact that God's self-sufficiency is exclusive to him means we cannot be self-sufficient. Although I listed all the ways that we are needy, there will be people in your congregation (probably between the ages of twenty and fifty) who have not quite figured that out yet. Remember the classic line "I'm Chevy Chase and you're not"? In this attribute, God proclaims, "I'm self-sufficient, and you're not." If we have not yet reached the ends of our individual capacity, we will soon enough. Put more accurately: if we have not realized that we are always operating at a deficit and that God is continually making up what we lack, then it's time to start acknowledging that reality.

Apply that as you speak it.

It may take you far more effort to apply theological constructs than, say, "Be anxious for nothing . . ." But know that your striving will be rewarded in the changed lives of your listeners.

Sermons on the Web

It is practically de rigueur for preachers to post videos of their sermons on the Internet. Even this little chapter will seem quaintly anachronistic. It provides a wonderful method of reaching a wholly different audience. Shut-ins, albeit technologically savvy ones, can access your church. Seekers too nervous to darken the door of your actual building can try you out from the anonymity of their home. Church shoppers can window shop on a Thursday and save a wasted Sunday morning. (And then come hear you instead.)

With all that wonderful opportunity, however, comes some dangers. Once up on the Internet, your sermon becomes immortal. It can be downloaded with copies disseminated a thousand ways to Sunday. Even if you take it off your site, it may already have started to be traded around the world at 176,000 miles per second.

So develop some rules. Remember that the congregation seated before you is not the only group of listeners. Make sure you provide enough detail to make sense of illustrations. Generally avoid being too "in-house." Be extra careful before you identify people by name, and get their permission to do so and insure that that they understand that your sermons are loaded onto the Internet.

If the above seems too difficult or too constraining, then set up some clear protocols for editing the recordings prior to posting on the web. What information needs to be redacted? Did anything happen unexpectedly so that some changes to the recording are necessary? In the coolness of a Monday morning, do you now realize that you phrased something in a manner that could be misunderstood or misconstrued? It would be better to have a slightly choppy, gappy audio file than to post something damaging to you or your flock, or worse, the kingdom.

Why Plagiarism Is Unnecessary

The web has created an unfortunate source of temptation for some pastors. Feeling the pressure to produce sermon after sermon every week, they succumb to yanking sermons off the Internet. I know folks from one church who were delighted to see their pastor's sermons improving week to week. They were becoming more interesting, rich with illustrations and application. Then they discovered that these were not their pastor's sermons after all.

His ministry was damaged for some time. Good came of it, though, as is God's way. The church had to examine itself as to why they were creating so much pressure, and the pastor developed a greater intimacy with the congregation. But for a while, the embarrassment was embarrassing for all of them.

Plagiarism is unnecessary for a number of reasons.

First, God called *you*, not The Reverend Perfect Sermon, to your church. He must have reasons why *you* are there. Mount the pulpit each Sunday with a confidence in his call on you and preach what he gives you for your congregation.

Second, sermons are manna for the day. As I discuss elsewhere, you are preaching this sermon for this congregation on this day. A sermon found on the Internet was preached for some other congregation, in some other place, with some other set of needs and abilities, on some other day. Sure there will be some overlap, but it won't be exactly what God wanted you to tell this congregation on this Sunday.

Third, I have written this book with the absolute, unshakable conviction that anyone called to the gospel ministry can learn to preach a reasonably good sermon. It may be difficult to move anyone from being a terrible preacher to the top ranks. But improvement to a level of reasonable competence is attainable for any preacher.

For Weddings and a Funeral

There are no events in the public life of an individual and family as deeply personal as weddings and funerals.

And, remarkably, no events elicit more trite, generalized, canned, and entirely impersonal sermons out of preachers. Every preacher has his wedding sermon and his funeral homily. Many don't bother to customize either one.

A wedding is a wonderful opportunity to speak to *this* couple about *their* lives together until they are parted by death. These two individuals have just vowed to take their entire persons and unite them with each other to create a team hopefully dedicated to the glory of God.

What a superb opportunity to speak to them personally. The most effective technique here is to direct your sermon to the bride and groom, while "allowing" the rest of the congregants to "listen in." Then weave in details about their lives, courtship, talents, professions, desires, and passions as you make your charge to the couple.

"Where will I get those details?" you may ask. Hopefully, you will not be meeting them for the first time at the end of the aisle all prettied up in white and tuxes. Two months before the wedding, have them fill out a survey or meet with them to ask them questions that will unlock some great specifics about their lives. What's your favorite food? Where did you go to school and what did you study? What's your job? What are you greatest joys in life? Which hobbies do you enjoy together and which are the ones you engage in apart from each other? What are your dreams for the future? How did you meet? What are the top three things you enjoy about each other? Why (in the world) do you want to marry him? Or her?

Now go and make that homily sparkle with its detail and intimacy. They'll never forget it, and the lessons you are trying to impart will stick like Velcro.

Although the timeframes are much more compressed, take the same opportunity with the deceased person's loved ones in preparing for a funeral. Learn about the person whose funeral you are shortly to conduct. Even if she's been a member of your church for fifty years and you've been there for eighteen of them, I guarantee there are things you don't know about her. Try to tease those out. Even posing the questions to the family members will be a ministry to them in their grieving. If you have ever lost someone dear to you, you probably wanted to reminisce with others about all the great attributes, funny habits, and memorable anecdotes of the deceased's life.

Your homily will be deeply meaningful to those assembled; and by showing that you care about and know details of the departed's life, you will demonstrate God's individualized and particular love for each of us.

The Jumping Judge and Alan Guy's Three-Step Leap onto the Stage

I tried a case before a judge aged forty-something and a jury of twelve of the commonwealth's finest citizens. Unlike most other judges, he virtually flew onto the bench each time he came into the courtroom. Vaulting a step or two, black robe flapping behind him, he evidenced a level of athleticism that easily translated into authority. The jury felt that things were well under control with that particular judge on the bench.

Years earlier, I had joined thirty-three hundred people packed into the huge old Armory in Wilkes Barre, Pennsylvania, to sing hymns. Some cultures climb greased poles. Others gather annually to drink beer. Still others run down cobblestoned streets in front of charging bulls. As you know by now, the Welsh sing hymns.

Although this Labor Day weekend provided other events, the hymn-singing festival was the apex. As was its custom, the hosting organization had hired a conductor (this one all the way from Wales) to lead the singing. Controlling that many voices took a great deal of skill and considerable energy. From his first movement, Alan Guy demonstrated that he was clearly up to the task.

Aside from his musical mastery, the one thing that struck everyone from the moment they first saw him was his dynamism. As he was introduced, he rose from his chair down below the stage and leaped onto the stage in a single bound.

Wearing a tuxedo, carrying his baton, he jumped all three steps! In that one action, he told us all that we needed to know about his preparedness and his enthusiasm for the commission.

How do you come into the sanctuary? How do you move from your chair on the platform to the pulpit? Do you walk? Shuffle? Stride? Stroll? What do you express in your physicality? Boredom? Fatigue? Ennui? Been here, done this? Or energy? Certainty of purpose? Desire? Palpable excitement about preaching the word of God to this people? Champing at the bit, desiring to go fifty furlongs all out? Go for the latter and watch the positive effect on your congregation.

Use of a Television Screen

Some (mega)churches use television screens or monitors to blow up the picture of the pastor. As seen from the back of the auditorium, the tiny figure of the preacher prowls the stage, with his image writ large to his right and left on the Jumbotrons hanging from the rafters. Talk about larger than life.

With the exception of churches that are so outsized that many would not be able to see their Lilliputian pastor any better than if he were a grasshopper, I don't think this is a good idea for the auditorium where the preacher actually is. I attended one church with about four hundred present, and the congregation spent more time looking at the Jumbotron than at the pastor standing right there in front of them.

Over time, this will lead to a loss of immediacy and intimacy, and the sermon becomes less participatory and more canned. We're simply too conditioned with what it means to watch TV. TV happens to us. We enter that semi-narcotic hypnotized state as the images flicker out at us. Sermons, on the other hand, are meant to involve our whole beings. We, although listening, are actively engaged in worship. Because I'm Presbyterian, I don't say "Amen" enough in church, but I'm sure never going to shout it at a plasma screen.

Preaching with Conviction

There are too many tributes that apply to Billy Graham to mention them all. He was a man of tremendous integrity, enviable humility, and deep empathy. But one of the greatest gifts that God gave him was a voice of conviction. The Spirit compelled belief, and Billy Graham's voice carried with it absolute certainty and confidence.

X Chromosomes (Part 2)

I have a couple of darling girls. Mari and Carys, even when both were under the age of five, already knew how to charm the opposite gender. As a result, they completely owned me. I didn't need anyone to warn me about future years. Neither of them will date until they are thirty-five.

I am also noting the distinct differences between them and my son. While they share a great deal in common, the girls experience their lives differently. They view the same episodes differently, and their reactions can be poles apart.

Years ago, their grandparents took all three to a Christmas pageant. When they came back, I asked Davey, who was nine at the time, what he thought of the show. "It was good," came the reply. End of story. Next, I asked Mari, who was four and half years old. Seven minutes later, I needed to interrupt her to ask for clarification on whether she had the ice cream during or after the intermission and if the angels actually flew across the stage.

How does this fit into preaching? I'm not entirely sure. But I know that somehow it must.

Your Face

It may be gloriously handsome. Drop-dead ugly. Nondescript. Pocked. George-Hamilton tanned. Generally serious. Naturally funny. Scarred. Welcoming. Oldish. Youngish.

Whatever it is, it's what we look at every Sunday morning for thirty minutes. It's the location from whence all your words are expelled.

And it can be a great help to you in communicating the gospel to us.

There is a comedian, Frank Caliendo, who is a master at impersonations. Many impersonators can do uncanny impressions of the voices of celebrities. Some even get a few hand gestures right, or some odd physical twitch or idiosyncrasy of the subject they are aping. But the best can actually contort their faces into looking like the man or woman. Mr. Caliendo is one of those latter few.

I can guarantee that the comedians don't just wake up one morning able to channel George Bush or John Madden. Instead, they spend a good deal of time in front of a mirror, bending, coaxing, cajoling, and otherwise working their facial muscles until the copy is striking and complete. Then they get on Jimmy Fallon's late night show and begin cashing in on all those hours.

Are you similarly aware of what your face looks like? If you are happy, how is that communicated by your face? Nervous? Concerned? Curious? I've been amazed at how little my face shows the smile I'm feeling. I may think that I'm radiating joy, but actually my face can appear quite passive. In the pulpit, that can be a liability, or an asset. I need to know this in order to make sure my facial expressions match what I am saying. If your face exhibits the same expression no matter what words are issuing from your mouth, then you are already starting the game behind by a touchdown and a field goal.

So let's play "Mirror, mirror on the wall, who's the most expressionless preacher of all?" for a few minutes. Look in a mirror. Don't worry, it's biblical (see James 1). Feel an emotion. Did it show up in the mirror? Say, "There is a balm in Gilead." Did the mirror agree? Proclaim, "There is no hidden corner of this orb of dirt to which the Hound of Heaven will not run to pursue you." Did your face reflect any of the intensity and urgency of that phrase? Run through a gamut of emotions and change your face to match each one. What is the mirror saying now? Who's winning, you or Mr. Spock?

I am not suggesting that you act. I deal with that danger in another chapter elsewhere in this book. What I am saying is that you should feel what you are saying and your face should cooperate with your gut to communicate those emotions.

Hirsute Homileticians

Given all that, let's talk beards. There are innumerable mothers who, upon meeting their daughter's shaggy dates for the first time, say, "Hey, what are you hiding with that facial hair?" With a beard, and sometimes even a mustache, you are essentially eliminating one of the most important tools of communication available to you: your face. It's not a whole lot worse than trying to preach without using conjunctions.

I can't tell if you're smiling. I can't tell if you have dimples. I can't tell if you are angry. Or sad. And those are just the extreme emotions and facial clues. What about wryness, quizzicality, pensiveness, or annoyance? Good luck showing those on your Grizzly Adams face.

I am well aware that Calvin and Arminius had beards. Spurgeon too. Beards also stubble their way in and out of fashion favor, depending on the decade (e.g., from the Van Dyke to the friendly mutton chop to the goatee or chinstrap). Perhaps if you are ministering in the Taliban-controlled regions of Afghanistan, you should wear a beard to blend in. But if you are preaching in a country populated with drugstores that sell Gillette Fusion Power Razors or Norelcos, then shave away the mask, my hairy friend.

Illustrations for Everyone

I've heard some preachers who draw every illustration from the universe of sports. Bit of a problem for the person in the pew who can't distinguish between an inning and a chukka.

At one point, my wife fell in love with a certain brand of jewelry. Apparently, some women enjoy getting together for "jewelry parties." I'd prefer to have sewing needles inserted into my nostrils. But they actually enjoy this, I am told. They gather together at a friend's home for dessert on a weekday evening. There will be no children present (they are at home with the befuddled fathers). There will be some food. But the focus will be several tables covered with velvet cloths and dozens of pieces of jewelry fashioned out of semiprecious stones and silver and gold. The women will ooh and ah, and if things go well for the host, they will deplete their family's bank account and each will come home with an anniversary gift for herself.

But you, happy preacher, if you are a man and your wife has this interest, find out all that you can about it. What attracts her to the jewelry? Why is it different from all the jewelry you have bought her? Why does she enjoy the evening? How is her experience of enjoyment shared by the other women? What's in it for her?

I have no immediate idea how any of that is going to help your preaching this Sunday, but I know it will eventually. By tuning in to the various constituencies of your congregation, you will begin the lifelong process of understanding your listeners. At some point, casually toss in a reference to "Stella & Dot jewelry," such as, "Even Solomon in all of his splendor, even if he had Stella & Dot jewelry, would not be arrayed as the lily of the field." Watch the sudden surge of interest in what you're saying. "The pastor just said Stella & Dot! I was invited to one of those parties just last week. How does he know about Stella & Dot?"

Inside the brain is the unarticulated, perhaps unformed thought: "Hmm, if he knows about Stella & Dot, he may actually know about me, and when he speaks from the Bible he may be able to apply it to my life directly." Pretty good outcome.

Dealing with the Compliments

When he stood at the door after preaching his heart out, people would often have some very nice things to say to my father. He would tell me that he would enjoy each compliment for the briefest moment and then "put them on a conveyor belt to heaven."

Keep Your Head Down

This is probably the most violated principle in all of public Scripture reading: When reading the Bible, do not look up until you have completed your task.

I attended a college convocation where several students and faculty had been chosen to read the Scripture text. They took their places each at their own microphone, holding portfolios with printed copies of their Gospel reading. For some reason, someone had decided that they should each take various bits and blips of the entire chapter. One would read one verse, then another three verses, and then two of them would read a phrase and so on. It was perfect if you simultaneously suffered from insomnia and were on your fifth Red Bull.

Compounding the problem was that one of the students had been assigned Jesus' words. Because he was about nineteen years old and lacked a beard, it was somewhat incongruous and added to the distraction. But the problems did not end there. This poor fellow was knee-bucklingly nervous as he stood in front of five thousand people—including all of his professors, many of his fellow students, and a number of dignitaries. His mouth was Death Valley desert dry, and the terror in his eyes made it appear that he was about to host the Oscars wearing a magenta tutu.

And then he eliminated any hope he had of getting through unscathed. As he started reading, he kept looking up, bobbing his head up and down, alternately reading a verse or two, and then looking vacuously into the darkness of the gymnasium as he finished a phrase. The actions overloaded his already overtaxed neurons. His brain simply could not retain the words he had just read, allow him to look up, continue speaking with his short-term memory-retained phrase, look back down, and seamlessly find where he now was supposed to be on his sheet of paper.

Oops, there's the first butchered word. Oops, now he can't find where his next phrase is on the paper. Oh dear, he said a word that's not even in the text. Phew, he just corrected himself. Oh no, now he said the same phrase twice—the first time while staring into the ether and then the second when he jumped back to find his spot . . . I don't think he realized that he just did that.

Never mind that it was a cringe to watch; what was far worse is that we could not concentrate on the Scripture.

Thus, brothers and sisters, the first reason why you should never look up while reading Scripture is because you absolutely, categorically cannot do it without messing it up in one of the ways that our poor undergraduate did. If you are a "looker-upper reader" and wish to refute me indignantly, please send me a DVD of you reading Scripture on three consecutive Sundays, and I guarantee I will be able to show you hesitations, slight gaps, and generally distracting nuances. All of which will have detracted from your essential task of reading God's very words to his people.

But there's an even more substantive reason for keeping your eyes on the Bible pages: Reading Scripture is not about you. This is not a performance where you get to sneak a peek at us to see if we're impressed with you. This is not a speech requiring eye contact to see if your audience is "getting it." You are not making up these words. You are reading what God has written. Scripture is entirely unique. You have the awesome privilege of uttering God's timeless communication to us. For that, it's best to keep your head down.

Visualization

When you describe something to the congregation, visualize it in your mind. Don't try to remember the fancy words you planned to use to describe your first car. Instead, see the car in your mind and describe it to us. Those fancy words will probably start coming back to you.

Non-visualization attempt:

> "We've all had those possessions, those things, that we loved. There's nothing necessarily wrong with that. In high school I had an old Buick. I really loved that car and remember a lot about it."

Great. I'm really riveted. I can almost smell the polyester carpet.

Visualization technique:

> "We've all had those possessions, those things, that we loved. There's nothing necessarily wrong with that. Mine was a '69 Buick with a 350-cubic-inch muscle car engine. She was two-tone with a dark brown roof sitting on a yellow body. The rear quarter panels had rusted out, so I bought some sheet metal, a rivet gun, Bondo, and matching yellow paint and then went to work. The result was pretty good, I must say. The interior was of the finest cracked vinyl upholstery, including a bench front seat (who sees those anymore?), and there was a short Dymo label strip with the word *Peace* punched onto it that had been stuck to the AC vent in the dashboard by the car's

first owner. And man, could she fly. Full throated, spin the rear wheels, guttural roar kind of flying."

In writing the above, I simply moved over the car's exterior and interior with my memory's eye—lovingly, I assure you—remembering the sight, sound, and smell of that beauty. The congregation is going to feel that passion as I speak. They are going to be able to think about the things that they love more easily as I detail that old '69 Buick.

Do the same as you describe anything from the pulpit. If you are depicting what you are visualizing, then the description will come alive and we will see it with you. You will end up remembering details that would otherwise have missed detection.

That Dymo strip came to mind only because as I typed this section, I was in that car, sitting in the driver's seat as a seventeen-year-old boy, firing up the beast. And that reference to a Dymo label is the kind of minutiae that make illustrations pop and give them their power and reality.

TED Tells Us We've Still Got It

Some people argue that the whole idea of standing in front of people for a half hour is hopelessly outdated and that our culture has moved away from such means of communication. If you want a successful church, you need to drop the sermon and focus on the praise band or discipleship or social justice. Nobody listens to lectures anymore.

TED says, "Hogwash!" TED's founder, Richard Wurman, decided to invite smart, creative people from around the world to stand on a stage for a maximum of eighteen minutes and tell a few million people about their coolest thing. These noteless, microphone-wearing, slide-show-remote wielding enthusiasts stride around the TED Talk stage, captivating their totally hip audience. Top topics include talks such as "The Surprising Science of Happiness," "Inside the Mind of a Master Procrastinator," and "The Art of Misdirection" (the latter given by "the greatest pickpocket in the world").

The audience listens raptly, laughs, is moved to tears, and experiences wonder, all while discovering things they never knew existed, the courtesy of someone talking at them.

TED has established the following mission: "TED is a global community, welcoming people from every discipline and culture who seek a deeper understanding of the world. We believe passionately in the power of ideas to change attitudes, lives and, ultimately, the world." All through lectures. Sounds curiously like the gospel of Jesus Christ. And preaching.

Since the first posted videos in 2006, people have viewed TED talks *billions* of times. Yes, that's with a *b*.

Hands Up (Part 3)

"Three of these chapters on hands?! What in the world! It can't be that important, can it?" you ask. Bear with me one last time.

Let's give all this stuff on "hands in the pulpit" a try. Right now, wherever you are in the privacy of your (study, office, bedroom, parked car, bathroom, etc.) use your hands (and if they so happen to come along for the ride, your arms, and the rest of your body) to convey the following to the imaginary audience before you.

Without speaking and by using only your hands, try communicating some of the following relative distances and dimensions:

Far far away
Near by
Deeper
Wider
Right here
Higher
Lower

How about sizes?

Teensy tiny
Ginormous
An average size
Thin
Fat
Great
Small

That's just charades, you say? Well, you couldn't play that game without using your hands, could you? So why would you try to preach without your hands? How about describing a few tangible things, again with your hands?

Chainsaw
Coffee cup
Mink coat (a fake one if you minister to PETA people)
The Alps
Rambunctious dog
Fax machine
Large comfortable easy chair
Chess game
Field mouse

Computer byte
Warm up by playing your air guitar
Turn on a lamp
Start the car
Shuffle a deck of cards
Use the TV remote control
Surf the web

Now we'll get into the challenging stuff. Still using one or both of your hands, experiment with the various emotions we all encounter and communicate them with your hands. Take the following abstract ideas and make your hands concretize them:

Peace
Love
Anger
Despair
Questions
Hope
Desire
Fear
Plenty
Want
Demand
Freedom
Uncertainty
Endless enjoyment

Point at an imaginary object. Mime the imaginary object. Mime the imaginary object to the imaginary object.

Object emphatically to miming to the imaginary object. With your hands.

Keep your hands high above your body for exalted, holy, wonderful, happy, gracious, or pure mentions.

Keep your hands low for despicable, deplorable, failed, ugly, sinful, base mentions.

Keep practicing throughout the day, if only to amuse your family, friends, or coworkers, or the lady in the car next to you at the light. Give your hands some experience in communication.

When you get in the pulpit this Sunday, take with you some visual cue and place it on the pulpit out of view of the congregation (perhaps a red 3x5 card, a pen, a bookmark, a yellow Post-it Note, or an anvil or a half-eaten banana). Then whenever you glance at that mnemonic device, do something with your hands that complementarily conveys the words that are passing your lips at that precise moment.

Now you're talking!

A Lot about Preaching Is Science

Science is replicable. You can mix an experiment one hundred times and you will always end up with the same result. Sermons, with a dozen cautions mostly having to do with the need for the Holy Spirit to precede and postcede your words, can have the same replicable properties.

Put another way, everyone called to the pulpit ministry can, through the adoption of a handful of principles of preaching, be a B preacher. Some may never be an A preacher, but there is absolutely no reason for them to remain C+ or worse. If some of the basic science were broken down, it would look like this:

- Preach from the Bible and choose your texts with intention.
- Study the Scripture closely, do your word studies, review other sermons and commentaries to make sure you are within orthodoxy, and make sure your points come from the text itself.
- Spend sufficient time meditating on the scriptural text you are going to preach so that the meanings become bonded to your soul and you preach something you have understood and lived on a deep level.
- Make sure the architecture of the sermon makes sense and addresses the major points of the text.
- Start your sermon well, using something interesting to seize your hearers' attention.
- Illustrate most if not all of your points. If it's a point worth making, it's worth illustrating.
- Choose illustrations that are new, fresh, unusual, personal, contemporary, real, and unexpected.
- Apply, apply, and apply. Apply as you go at each point made, and don't wait until the end of the sermon.
- Have a point to your sermon and let the congregation in on it.
- Finish, don't fizzle. Quit while you're ahead, not when they're dead.

That's a guaranteed B sermon. Perhaps even a B+. And that's good enough to keep them coming back for more.

Illustrations Are the Delivery System for Propositional Truths

They are the hypodermic needle injecting the meaning deep into our souls. Since we can't attach God's word to our foreheads, illustrations become the Superglue for truths. They are the Stickum on the pole vaulter's hands. The carrier pigeon with the verses tied to its feet. The town crier shouting out the day's news. The adhering part of the Post-it Note . The . . . well, you get the idea.

Athletes Repeat the Same Action Over and Over until It Is Natural, Unforced, Reliable

In some ways, your preaching should be that way.

Nerves

I have friends who hate speaking or performing publicly. They fret and worry in the days leading up to the occasion. They have sweaty palms, jumpy stomachs, and fitful sleep when called upon to participate in a public event. This can be particularly so if they are preaching, singing, or otherwise leading in the worship of God's people. Will the congregation like the sermon? Will they like the illustrations? Will they find it all very exciting? Will they think well of the preacher? Will he or she be asked back?

If given the opportunity, I make a special point to tell them that, at the end of the day, "It's all about you." This is most especially true when it comes to leading worship. When they are preaching, they should be continually thinking: "What do people think about me?" "Do they find me funny?" "Am I as good as the guy who preached last week?" "Are my ideas so profound that everyone will think 'Hey, that guy's so profound'?" "Do they like my hair?" and "How do they like my new suit?"

I jest. It is not, of course, about you. It is about him.

As a youngster, I once asked a woman who often sang beautiful solos during worship whether she got nervous before the service. She said she generally did not and that nervousness was an indication of a sinful attitude of pride. I thought that was a pretty obnoxious, self-righteous, even pompous response. Until I realized that in good part, she was right. Now, that is not to say that nervousness is solely a product of sinful pride. Most public speakers experience some jitters. And as I address elsewhere, the task of preaching is an awesome one that in a real sense should terrify. But if your nervousness is adversely affecting your performance and even ability to do the task at all, then you should check your heart.

Never forget that you are preaching because God has called you to the task. Relax and lean on him to take your imperfect words and efforts and to redeem and to convert them into Words of Life to your hearers.

The Rest of the Service

A worship service without a sermon is like a Philly steak and cheese sub without the beef. Sure, the roll is nice and hot cheese is pleasant, but "where's the beef?!" We must be equally quick to note that a Philly steak and cheese sub without a chewy roll, cheese, mushrooms, and onions, and a hearty serving of ketchup-drenched French fries on the side is also missing something. (This analogy fails entirely on a nutritional level, but humor me.)

A Philly steak and cheese sub made with parmesan cheese, Dijon mustard, and pumpernickel toast points, however, also fails to hit the mark. Those ingredients—mustard, parmesan cheese, and pumpernickel toast points—are wonderful food items in the right culinary context but, for most people, simply do not go well with a hot steamy steak and cheese sub.

Certainly, the rest of the worship service is not just "other stuff" to fill in the time around the sermon. Conversely, however, we ought not to view those worship elements as standalone activities with no connection to each other or the sermon.

Keep in mind your primary theme and sermon points when you choose the hymns and worship songs. I am perplexed when I hear of pastors who delegate the choice of music completely to their organist or other music leaders without any conversation about the substance of the sermon. I am only slightly less amazed when preachers, who lack even a smidge of musical ability, insist on choosing hymns and then do so purely for lyrical content without any concern for the absolutely unsingable melody "embracing" the words. Work with your musicians to find the hymn tunes and words that accomplish effective worship and complement the theme of the day.

Naturally, if your church has an extended contemporary worship period at the start of the service—say, seven to eight songs—not every song will buttress your sermon text and theme. But some reasonable attempt to reflect the theme in the voiceovers or a song or two will serve to enrich the worship time as a whole.

Prayers of confession and intercession can incorporate the sermon's emphases. So too can the benediction. Why say every single week of the year: "May the Lord be with you, may he make his face to shine upon you and may he grant you . . ." when instead you can seamlessly work the week's theme into the last words you speak to your flock? Make it fresh. Don't let our minds wander as you deliver your customary benediction. Pray God's grace on us as he applies his—(insert the truth you just preached)—to our lives.

For giggles, change things around from time to time. Put the cheese under the meat or slide the fries into the bun, just to keep us on our toes.

Who's the Bogeyman? Identifying and Addressing the Primary Opposition

There are times when we just can't hear what you're saying. Why is that?

There will be blockages to the particular sermon you are crafting for this Sunday. As you work on it, you should anticipate the kinds of opposition that you might receive that arise from the topic or text itself. Your analysis will take some creativity.

Here are some diagnostic questions that might help you get into our minds as listeners:

1. Is the biblical event in question actually historical?
2. Is the story easily believable from a scientific perspective?
3. How do we know that the passages were not dated after the events described?
4. Will some of the hearers feel excluded, because they will assume the message does not apply to them?
5. Could some of the people who will be hearing the message have suffered a trauma or hold a negative view due to some personal experience that will keep them from accepting the truths?

Some examples may help.

1. Noah. I can guarantee that 10 percent of us and maybe more are just wondering whether the flood covered the *whole* earth. How was that possible? Where did the water come from? Why didn't it just run into holes created by volcanoes? Isn't the story really just metaphorical? Or did it actually happen? Or does "whole earth" mean something more local?
2. Same with Jonah. Three days inside a whale? That's a true fish story, isn't it? Or is it?
3. God as our Father. If you preach a sermon for Father's Day or any other time of the year that seeks to flesh out God's relationship to us as our Father, then you had better consider some of the following likely scenarios.
   - "My father was not a bad man but had been beaten down by life, working a dead-end job. He came home every night at 5:35 p.m. for dinner and then went into the den and watched television until 10:00 p.m. I don't ever remember seeing him laugh."
   - "My father came home drunk every night and beat me and my brother and my mother and then passed out on the living room couch."
   - "My father sexually abused me from age six until I left the home to go to college."
   - "My father was (incompetent, geeky, unkind, rash, angry, ineffective, unworthy, dishonest, ugly, fat, undisciplined, manipulative, unattractive, pitiable, powerless, disrespected, wore a bad hair weave, untalented, boring, weird, embarrassing, handicapped, had undiagnosed ADD, etc.).

How are you going to preach a sermon on God as Father to these people?

The answers start jumping out immediately. God is the paragon of fatherhood. God defines what it means to be a good father. It is precisely our own fathers' failings and shortcomings that point us to our Father God. And so on.

Your sermon will not be as effective if you have not thought about what might keep us from hearing you. Tackle those impediments head on, and we will experience an overpowering sense of relief. And we may even draw near to the truth with an added vulnerability.

Context Is King

Keep in mind the most basic principles of biblical exegesis: Please don't cherry-pick a verse to make your point. A verse should be understood in the context of the paragraph. A paragraph should be understood in the context of the chapter. A chapter should be understood in the context of the whole book. The book must be understood in the context of the whole Bible.

Your Job: To Be Huge and Invisible

In some ways, you really must achieve what would seem to be an impossible task. Success is in some ways measured by the sincerity of the worship. Can you direct us to worship the Lord? Ironically, the only way to do that is to be a large presence in the pulpit. We must look intently at you, watching and following your every word, as if you are the conductor.

But here's the kicker: You must also be invisible. We need to be able to look at you and follow you *while seeing only God*, hearing those profound and arresting words, illustrations and ideas out of your mind, while he imprints the truths contained therein on our hearts and in the DNA of our souls.

That's your task as a preacher. With all your fiber and being and ability, preach the word. Of course, we should want to hear you. Of course, we should come expecting great things. Of course, you will do your best each week.

But never forget: It's all about God.

How to Be an Absolutely Irrelevant Bore

I recently went to a church excited to hear a preacher I had not heard before, who was covering for the pastor who was away on vacation. He started with all the nice comments about being pleased as punch to be provided the opportunity to preach in this prominent pulpit, and so on. Then he pulled out page one of his sermon. When he had finished reading that page, he turned to the second page and read that page. Then as he reached the end of that page, he turned the page and read page three. Occasionally, he would look up and do what appeared to be a little freelancing. But I soon realized that he was just saying the words that were printed before him. Half the time that he looked up, he would forget a word or two. The other times, he would look back down and be unable to find where he was reading immediately, creating awkward silences.

Perhaps the best way to demonstrate the ineffectiveness of this approach to preaching is to picture us all sitting there, beads of perspiration forming on our foreheads, as he stumbled and, I kid you not, misread his own manuscript using the wrong word, not once, not twice, but *three* times in rapid succession until he found his place again.

Why read a manuscript? Why not just hand out copies and let the congregation go home twenty-five minutes early?

"Manuscripterists" seem to be more concerned about *how* they are saying something than *what* they are saying. They want to get the words right, the turn of phrase correct, and make the vocabulary rich. With a bit more effort, they could accomplish all those worthy desires without a manuscript.

You may argue: "I'm scared that if I don't use my manuscript, I'll plumb forget my sermon."

No, you won't.

My mother, as a newlywed, accompanied my father to the graduation ceremony for a Midwestern college. The gymnasium was packed with over sixty-five hundred students, faculty, parents, and friends. My father was to give the commencement address. The school had some Dutch history and many of the faculty, including the president, were of Dutch descent. That matters only because they were tall. Exceptionally tall. And my father most decidedly was not.

As the processional came in, here came the president and the other dignitaries, bringing up the rear and towering above my father. My mother was struck with a certain terror by the scene and turned to the president's wife, with whom she was seated, and asked, "Do you get nervous for your husband?" The wife answered quickly, "Oh no, never. My husband has everything he needs to say today written out in that folder he's carrying." My mother blanched as she realized that her little Gwyn carried nothing but his brain with him.

But she had no reason to fear. My father knew *what* he wanted to say.

When teaching, my father would require his students to preach without any notes at all, not just without a manuscript. I'm sure that learning to preach without a net built up the confidence of those young preachers. I don't know, however, that it is a necessity on a permanent basis. Having an outline with you in the pulpit can be helpful.

But wean yourself from the word-for-word manuscript. Take up detailed notes. Then just bullet points. Then just a 3 x 5 card with a couple of points. Perhaps one week do a triple somersault with no net. What's the worst that could happen?

Don't worry, it won't.

The Proof Is in the Homiletic Pudding

Despite me being only a lawyer, a couple of good friends asked me if I would officiate at their wedding. Massachusetts issues one-day licenses for just that purpose. I had been terribly busy, and with only three days to go before the Saturday ceremony, my homily was unstructured, cobbled together, clichéd, and, above all else, *unremittingly* boring. With many of the attendees probably lacking in much biblical knowledge, I had chosen to speak on Jesus' first miracle in Cana where he changes the water into wine. The chosen wedding order of service made reference to the miracle, and I thought it would be reasonable to flesh it out a little. My three points:

1. God thinks marriage is fun.
2. God takes marriage seriously.
3. God helps us in our marriages.

I realized on Wednesday that my points absolutely stunk. And, worse, they and I were violating everything for which this book stands.

For starters, I hadn't really meditated on the text. So I began reading it in earnest. I started seeing details I had not noticed before. Jesus *and his disciples* were attending. I'd always seen Jesus' presence there as just happenstance. I had assumed he was probably a friend of the family, sitting with all the other guests. Now I began to see that he may have been an honored guest, a rabbi starting his ministry, already collecting disciples. Some further textual study backed that up.

That, in turn, led me to wonder whether the fact that he was an honored guest was what created the motivation for his mother to ask for his intervention. I doubt she was expecting him to turn water into wine. Instead, perhaps she felt it would be his gracious response to the hosting calamity that could have a salutary effect on the other guests. If he, the rabbi, didn't get angry about the perceived slight of insufficient wine, then his guests would take their cue from him.

Instead, Jesus was transformational. He didn't solve the problem in the way anyone would have expected. And that's still how he works. He comes in to our marriages and changes things, changes us. He transforms.

Perhaps you do not like my interpretation. Fine. I know we can agree that Jesus transforms, so I didn't lead my flock for the day completely astray. But more importantly, the interpretation came from really pondering and ruminating on the text. I had finally let it settle in to my marrow.

Next, what to do about these titles? Ugh. Three points of miasma. Not a chance in the galaxy that any of the guests would remember them a month later, including me. The only rhyming word is God, so that doesn't count.

Seven minutes of twiddling and experimenting and talking to my wife, and I shrunk it to two simple points and a tagline:

Marriage Is Pro-Fun.

Marriage Is Profound.

"Jesus Keeps the Party Going."

Next, I wove in the meaning of the names of the couple. In this case, the bride's first name could mean "my God is abundance" and the husband's surname meant "by the thorns." The former I injected into the Pro-Fun section by encouraging the groom to enjoy the abundance of joy his wife would provide to their marriage. The latter I incorporated into the Profound discussion by talking about the fact that marriage will experience the pricks of thorns from time to time.

Throughout it all, I repeated the tagline: "Jesus keeps the party going."

Now, for my final tweak. I had been to the location of the outside wedding, on a patio, next to a kidney-shaped pool with gorgeous rockscaping and landscaping carved into the surrounding hillside. The ceremony was going to be classy and fancy with beautiful floral arrangements and a professional harpist and violinist serenading the couple from a gazebo overlooking the assembled throng.

So I grabbed a neon-orange five-gallon plastic Home Depot bucket.

In the middle of my sermonette, I reached behind the rock fire pit and pulled out that sucker and made my point. I asked if they had noticed that Jesus pointed to five to six jars, each holding twenty-five to thirty gallons of water. God was bountiful in blessing this wedding. That was a whole lot of wine. In fact, it was thirty of these Home Depot buckets' worth! Pro-fun, baby.

My closing sentence: "When you're both sitting together on the porch of the extended care residence, rocking in your chairs, my prayer is that you will look into each other's eyes, turn up your hearing aids, and say: "Our marriage was and is pro-fun, our marriage was and is profound, and through it all, Jesus kept the party going."

I leave to those in attendance to decide whether it was a good sermon. I can judge, however, that it was immeasurably better than the absolute yawner that was ready for delivery on Wednesday. Sometimes it's the last two hours of sermon preparation that makes all the difference.

The "Problem" of Too Much Scripture

I've been in the pew for sermons where we were treated to a trip through the pastor's concordance. It seemed that the preacher prepared his sermon from the middle column of his Scofield Bible, chasing one verse and book after another until we were all frantically flipping pages, playing an adult game of Bible Sword Drill. We may have been impressed with his breadth of knowledge of the Scriptures. But we also left with paper cuts and cramps in our fingers and forgot what the main text was about.

I think this impulse arises out of a misunderstanding of the oral medium.

In legal briefing, we lawyers use a writing mechanism called "string citing." And it's a very helpful tool when used in the right context. For example, let's say a lawyer argues to the court that his client church has a right to build a sanctuary with a one hundred and fifty foot steeple. He will research the cases in his home state first to find ones that support his position. He might also look to any of the other forty-nine states to see if others have cases that are helpful to his argument. He will then insert in his brief a long string of citations that would include the case names, the numbers of the volumes and pages where each case is reported, and a parenthetical phrase outlining the facts and the court's conclusion in each case. To be fair, he would also include references to cases that are unhelpful to his argument and then seek to distinguish them from his church's situation. Doing so, as you might imagine, makes for a long document.

When the court reads the attorney's brief, the judge can, in the privacy of her chambers, pull up each of the cases cited, read them, ponder them, and decide whether the church's reliance was justified.

But when that lawyer comes into court to argue the case face to face with the judge, he will not refer to all those other cases. It is simply not the forum. Instead, he will spend the largest proportion of his time in court fleshing out his church's building intentions, pointedly referring to one or two of the cases most helpful to his position to undergird his oral argument. It is certain that the judge will not ask questions about a dozen cases either. The judge will focus mostly on the client's situation and perhaps colloquy with the attorneys on a case or two.

Therein lies the difference between the written document and the oral presentation. The point of each is to persuade and educate. But each forum and medium dictates far different approaches.

So too in preaching. Preaching is not a written article. Preaching is not Sunday school.

Trust the pericope: if you chose it, go for it! The multiverse quoting technique is often an indication of a preacher who is not sure that his chosen text can support a whole sermon. You have picked out that specific passage of Scripture with its peculiar length, context, and placement in the Bible. Now make it sing for us.

Plumb it to the depths. Ask the who, what, where, why, and how questions. Who is mentioned? Who is speaking? To whom? About whom? What is the context? What is the substance of what is being said, written, or declared? What type of Scripture is this (historical, narrative, poetic, prophetic, apocalyptic, didactic, etc.)? What comes before? What comes after? What point or points is the writer making? What is the connection to Christ's work? Where is the text? Where are the people involved in the text? Where else does this story or principle appear (careful, though, for we're just getting a better sense of *this* passage)? Why did the people do what they did and say what they said? How does this passage fit within the greater context of the Bible itself, God's work of redemption, God's character, and God's purposes for his people? What parallels do you find in our everyday life? What are the main points? How can you illustrate them? What is this passage intended to do to us? For us? With us? What are we supposed to do now? Obviously, these are just a few of the questions you should be asking of the text. But by attacking the pericope with this level of enthusiasm and diligence, you will encounter a richness in your text that is not always immediately apparent.

Enjoy the great advantages to going deeper in the text. You will be teaching us the richness of Scripture, as we will see just how profound each passage is. Sometimes the best nutrition is in the marrow of the bone; many preachers never get there, content instead to nibble at the hard surface a few times before moving on to another carcass. Your approach will help bring Scripture alive for the congregation and demonstrate that there is something for everybody in God's word. Even mature Christians will be more likely to capture a glimpse of something to ponder anew.

"Going deeper" captures the best aspect of expository preaching, ensuring that you preach the whole counsel of God. You will be celebrating the opulence of each text, while avoiding the problem of personal themes and favorite topics. If you quote too many texts, you much more easily fall into the trap of treating a particular passage as merely a springboard to "something else." "Going deeper" keeps us truer to the authorial intent for that specific Scripture. It also makes preaching the rest of the book less likely to be repetitive.

For example, if you address 1 Peter 2:18–25 as simply and generally a section on Christians bearing up under suffering, then where are you going to go in a few weeks when you hit 1 Peter 3:8–22?

> [18]Slaves, submit yourselves to your masters with all re-
> spect, not only to those who are good and considerate,
> but also to those who are harsh. [19]For it is commendable
> if a man bears up under the pain of unjust suffering be-
> cause he is conscious of God. [20]But how is it to your credit
> if you receive a beating for doing wrong and endure it?
> But if you suffer for doing good and you endure it, this
> is commendable before God. [21]To this you were called,
> because Christ suffered for you, leaving you an example,
> that you should follow in his steps. [22]"He committed no
> sin, and no deceit was found in his mouth." [23]When they
> hurled their insults at him, he did not retaliate; when he
> suffered, he made no threats. Instead, he entrusted him-
> self to him who judges justly. [24]He himself bore our sins in
> his body on the tree, so that we might die to sins and live
> for righteousness; by his wounds you have been healed.
> [25]For you were like sheep going astray, but now you have
> returned to the Shepherd and Overseer of your souls.

First Peter 2:18–25 seems to focus on suffering in the workplace, or at least it uses that as a starting point. If you ignore 1 Peter 2:18, or simply use it as a springboard to a broad discourse on suffering, you will be giving short shrift to the often enormous challenges to those of us who live out our faith at our jobs and have to deal with the suffering that can follow.

And if you've been too general, when you hit Peter's treatment of suffering in the third chapter, your congregation will think it's déjà vu all over again and that they've already heard this sermon once before. In fact, you may be tempted to just skip over 1 Peter 3:17 ("It is better, if it is God's will, to suffer for doing good than for doing evil"), because you may feel that you've already addressed Christian suffering. Worse, you may have already bundled the two texts in the first sermon and have now missed an opportunity to demonstrate the nuances of the word to your congregation. God and Peter saw the importance of both passages. It's a safe bet to join them by explaining the distinction.

Run deep.

So, When Should You Refer to a Scriptural Text That Is Not the One on Which You are Preaching?

Your first and last instinct should be to stay with the Scripture you chose for today's sermon. Are you sure that you've explained it thoroughly, illustrated it creatively, and applied it effectively?

If your answer is yes, then here are some suggestions. It helps us if you quote other texts in the following situations:

1. Where the main text concerns the fulfillment of a biblical prophecy.
2. Where the main text refers to or quotes another portion of Scripture.
3. Where the main text introduces an apparent contradiction.
4. Where the main text creates confusion.
5. Where you intend to introduce a distinction between your main text and other treatments of the subject matter elsewhere in Scripture. For example, in preaching on Paul's treatment of marriage in 1 Corinthians 7, you might point out the differences from what he writes in Ephesians 5.
6. Where the text is missing a point. But take care here. Apparently, God did not put it in that specific text, so perhaps neither should you.
7. Where you are unable to teach a text's critical point directly out of the main text alone.
8. Where there is not enough to the text alone. Caution again here. I do not mean this to be a catchall exception large enough for a Sword Drill bus. If you think this exception applies, perhaps your pericope does not have enough points and you should just expand your selection.

When done well, citing other Scripture can have beneficial effects. It can help the congregation see the unity of God's word and increase our confidence in God's word. It can provide some real clarity to the main text. It can impress upon us the desirability and profitability of broad Scripture study.

But it more easily has its downsides. It can unwittingly teach the congregation that Scripture is "thin" and that there is not enough meat in any one text to fill a full twenty-five minutes. If you don't show us how you dig for treasures, then we'll never learn the beauty of that endeavor.

In fact, the opposite actually happens, because Scripture is not thin. Thus, and most unfortunately, by introducing a new text you may end up inviting a whole new set of questions and problems without having or taking the time to resolve them. For example, if we are delightfully buried deep in a parable and you give a passing reference from Isaiah without fleshing it out, then we all start thinking about Isaiah and his prophecies. Some of us won't remember the details of the allusion, some of us won't know where Isaiah is in the Bible, and some of us will head down an unprofitable prophet rabbit trail as we try to follow your thinking.

Avoid referring to other scriptural texts if all it does is say the same thing. Avoid it if there is only a thematic similarity with your main text. Avoid it if you are doing so only to impress your hearers with your biblical knowledge.

I occasionally enjoy a trip to an art museum. Most of the time, I move with relative purpose but quickly, from painting to painting. I may cover a dozen rooms with several hundred paintings in a couple of hours. Then on to lunch and some shopping with the gang. But occasionally, I have done what is recommended by those who understand art. I have sat down in front of a masterpiece and just looked at it. Stared at it with intensity. Let my mind wander and return to it. Noted the painter's use of light, color, brushstroke, medium, and subject matter. I've sat there for ten or fifteen minutes, an eternity for a Type A like me. And over the course of that time, I've begun to see wondrous details I never saw in my sixteen-seconds-a-painting art museum excursions. Beyond all, however, I've been washed over by the beauty and power of the work and have wondered at the skill, intention, and passion of the artist.

Good preaching from a single scriptural text accomplishes the same.

Going to School on Other Preachers

Nothing wrong with learning from great preachers. Or reading their books. Or even adopting things you see in others that you think are effective. But remember that adoption is fundamentally different from imitation. It's perfectly fine that Franklin Graham or Ann Graham Lotz evoke some of the style of their father, Billy. It's in the genes. It would, however, be weird if one of their ministry staff did so. It would be positively bizarre if you did.

When you adopt something, do so to improve your instrument, not to try to become someone else's.

Using What's Handed to You

There was a television show, *MacGyver*, in which the hero was distinctly known for being able to beat the bad guys and get himself out of the most awkward and dangerous situations by using whatever was at hand. Unlike James Bond who early in every movie spent ten minutes with "Q" getting outfitted with exploding pens, laser watches, cars that shoot torpedoes, and eyeglasses with metal-cutting torches (all which would figure prominently later in the movie), MacGyver would achieve the same utility out of a clothes hanger, chewing gum, a Raggedy Ann doll, and a shoelace. He wasn't reaching for pre-planned gizmos. No, he'd just grab whatever was at hand. His name has become a verb, as in "MacGyver your way out of a mess."

Sometimes preachers get the same opportunity to reach around their surroundings and use it to drive home a point.

At a missions conference I attended, the Saturday evening session was in progress when the chairperson of the hosting missions committee, as was her custom, went to the pulpit to introduce all the visiting missionaries. As she called out their names and described their work, each one came forward to join the others in a long line across the sanctuary. The group included both foreign missions and local outreach folks. When she came to a relatively new local ministry, a half-way house, she suddenly stopped and, with a good deal of personal embarrassment, had to admit that she had only just met the woman who was representing the organization. The blushing chairwoman blurted, "I'm embarrassed to say but I've forgotten your name. I left it in my Bible in the other building. Would you please tell us your name?"

At least a half hour later, the visiting pastor was well into preaching his second sermon of the weekend. He had chosen Luke 10 where Jesus sends out the seventy-two to preach the gospel in the surrounding communities. The disciples had gone out in pairs to spread the news that Jesus was coming. In doing so, they had encountered opposition, some of it demonic. When they returned, they were tickled pink as they described to Jesus that even the demons had submitted to them in Jesus' name!

Jesus was full of joy as he heard them each report back on their trips, essentially telling them that "you haven't seen anything yet. Don't rejoice at demons being cowed. Rejoice because that's nothing compared to the fact that your names are written in heaven! You guys are in the Book of Life." That's the payoff of this life. That's the driver of missions. That's the enormous source of excitement for the Christian. Whatever happens here, our names are written permanently above.

Then the preaching mastery came.

> "Do you remember our chairwoman, Stephanie, introducing all our missionaries earlier this evening? She's great at it, she's a pro. But she hit a snag, and Stephanie said she couldn't remember Barbara's name. And as she asked Barbara to identify herself, Stephanie apologized for the mistake of leaving her Bible in the other building and because, as she explained to us—and how rich is this?!—she had written Barbara's name on a note *in her Bible*! Listen folks, it doesn't matter if nobody remembers your name here on earth. *Your name is written in the Book of Life!*"

Bang! Pow! Shazzam! He'd just taken a moment handed to him, a moment that Stephanie might have otherwise rued for the rest of the conference. He sucked all the embarrassment out of it and transformed it into an illustration that none of us will soon forget.

Another Great Illustration

Some years back, I had the privilege of hearing Dr. Bryan Chapell, a preacher who is particularly gifted in illustrating his points. In one sermon, he was trying to sell us on God's love as a heavenly Father for us his children, as sinful as we are. He described a time that he and his boys were on a trip, and he warned them not to go near a particularly dangerous drop. But being of the young male persuasion, the temptation proved overpowering and climb near the danger they did. Of course, one of them fell down the steep sides of the embankment. Panicked, his brothers ran to get their father, who immediately rushed to the edge of the steep hill. Without waiting an instant, Bryan plunged down the side, into the muck and dirt at the bottom, and wrapped his arms around his bleeding son. He climbed out, covered with mire and blood, and took to tending his boy. Bryan did not think for a moment about any danger to himself, nor did he hesitate to embrace his son, covered with blood and grime. Then he brought the illustration home. Such is God's passion for us, even in our sinful state. Passionate. The love of a father for a boy shown by the picture of a bleeding, mud-spattered dad bear-hugging his son mirrors God's love for us far better than this sentence ever could. And that's the power of an effective illustration.

Muse on the details Bryan provided. He set up the innocent trip, a family out for fun together. He provided the warning. We could see what was coming next. He described the danger and then the boy's temptation, disobedience, and resulting injury. He then increased the pace of the illustration, rushing through his actions, overcome by the passionate love of a father. And finally, he gave us the denouement, the child safe in his father's arms, and a father who had come down to mix in his wayward child's dirt.

Expository Preaching: The Real Kind

True expository preaching seeks to communicate the truths of Scripture, not to showcase the original language skills of the preacher. We expect that you have spent some time in the Greek. We trust that you have a good grasp of how the critical words are used elsewhere in Scripture and perhaps even in secular writings of the time. We imagine that you have read other commentators' views on certain translation problems. We accept that you are aware of the various interpretive choices you are forced to make.

But we're not going to need to know all of that to figure out how to apply your passage to our lives this coming week. We need to hear what the writer meant when he wrote what he did. We need to know what changes God intends to make in our lives as a result of hearing his word. We need to know about God, not the diphthong.

For example, careful exegesis of Hebrews 12:1 uncovers an important distinction between *things* that *hinder* and *sins* that *entangle*. In fact, it is a difference that is easily missed if we focus only on the English. Those things that hinder can be otherwise perfectly acceptable things such as sports, hobbies, and other interests. But they may keep us from running the race well. On the other hand, there are sins that entangle us, resulting in the same hindrance. Too often, people see only the sin angle and miss that we may need to curtail "good" things in our lives if they are keeping us from success in the race.

But we don't need to be told the distinction in the Greek to make that sermon captivate our hearts. In fact, we'd probably end up confused and distracted. Far better for the preacher to split his sermon into two sections when attacking verse 1 of Hebrews 12 and park his preaching car there for a good deal of time. Suddenly, the text will come alive as we all realize there is a whole new category of things that may be having an adverse effect on our running abilities. We are all then the beneficiaries of his expert exegesis, without ourselves having to be experts in exegesis.

True expository preaching takes the skeleton of the exegesis and word studies and fleshes it up with the sinews, muscles, and fat of illustrations. It dresses that sermonic body with the attractive clothing of well-tailored applications. In the beautifully arrayed expository sermon, the flaunting of a dozen Greek words is usually as incongruous as a compound fractured bone protruding from a tuxedo. It's jarring. Even a bit painful.

True expository preaching trusts the text to provide the substance of the sermon and then illustrates and applies it creatively and beautifully.

A Girl Named Beasley: Children's Sermons Done Right

Hands down, the best children's sermons I ever heard were by a young seminarian who was doing an internship at my home church. Over a period of *months*, he gave the children's sermon every week, and every week he captivated *everyone*. Every Sunday, we all looked forward to hearing about Beasley's latest adventure.

I've tried to figure out why every week's sermon worked so well.

First, every sermon focused on Beasley. We learned to love this little spunky redheaded girl. We came each week wondering what she had done rightly or wrongly in the last few days. Beasley occasionally misbehaved. And other times, she acted with virtue. But at all times, she acted normally. The first week was fine. The second was pleasant. But by the third week, we were hooked on Beasley.

Second, each story had a clear but not clichéd point based on a biblical truth. Too often, children's sermons sound more like Aesop's fables than scripturally founded lessons. Beasley's peradventures resulted in an application of God's word not subtly but artfully.

Next, each story spoke truths to both the kids sitting up front on the floor at our intern's feet and to the adults back in the pews. It was this last aspect that made them hit the trifecta. The children's sermon is aimed at the kids, naturally. And the important goal must be to communicate a truth to the children that they can then incorporate into their lives and write upon their hearts.

But our intern never forgot that he had another few hundred adults sitting and listening with attention to his sermon. Without playing to the adults, an all too often temptation, he would throw in a quip or a remark that connected to the adults far more readily than the kids. But the kids did not know it. There's an old chestnut about children's sermons that captures the essential challenge of the task:

Preacher: "Hi kids, what's gray, lives in trees, and has a big bushy tail?

Kid: "Sounds like a squirrel, but I'm going to go with 'Jesus.'"

Most children's sermons are targeted to about that level of biblical and theological sophistication. The answer to every question is either God or Jesus. And the kids know it. So how likely is it that any of them is going to listen? And even if they do, how are they going to learn?

When my son was old enough to want a made-up story at bedtime, I knew I was in trouble. How could I make up stories night after night after night? I then realized that my task would become immeasurably simpler if I developed an ongoing story with multiple adventures and a consistent cast of characters. So were born Frick and Frack, who happened to be a couple of years older than Davey, my boy. They had a magic world they would occasionally visit where all kinds of fun things awaited. But they also went to school, church, and anywhere else around town. They often had experiences curiously similar to the ones Davey was encountering in all those different places. There was still a need for some creativity, but I was not writing a new movie with a new cast of characters every night. Beasley's lesson lived on in my kids' bedtimes.

Go Anywhere

Are there places you should not preach? If invited, should you preach in a mosque? If invited, should you preach in a casino? If invited, should you preach in a bar? The funeral of an avowed atheist?

Preach anywhere. Make only one stipulation and consider it nonnegotiable: You will never compromise your message. If they are willing to hear what you have to say, then feel free to accept the invitation. If they seek to limit what you can say, water down the gospel, turn your message into a pan-religious ecumenism, then turn it down. But if you can preach freely, preach anywhere.

My father once preached at a Jewish funeral. About Christ. It turns out that the decedent had a love for Welsh hymns. So my father wove the texts of great Welsh hymns throughout his sermon. Those attending all thought they were hearing about their loved one's cultural interests. In that setting, the hymns became Trojan horses filled with saving eternal truths.

What he recognized was that he had been invited as a minister of the gospel of Jesus Christ. Not as an orator. Not as a white-haired man with a cool Welsh accent. Not as a pal. But as one of God's preachers. So that is how he would go.

God Constantly Illustrates

God knows that we need illustrations to appropriate truths to our core. God is still illustrating himself in the world. "The heavens declare . . ."

Old Preachers Never Die

Prior to his cancer, there were only two times in fifty years of preaching ministry that my father missed an engagement. The first was in the Blizzard of '69 when ten-foot snowdrifts stalled (but did not prohibit) his eventual arrival to preach. The second, twenty-five years later, was due to a brief illness when his doctor prevailed upon him not to preach that one Sunday morning (he'd actually passed out unconscious on Saturday). He preached numerous times when he had the flu, once with mononucleosis (he took three days to get over it), once with a broken thumb (broken that morning when he fell off the horse he was riding to get to the church in the nether regions of some mountainous terrain), and on more than a few occasions with laryngitis (he'd pray and it would always clear up just for the sermon).

But by the summer of '93, the cancer had invaded his bones, and with the greatest of reluctance, we prevailed upon him to cancel all of his preaching engagements. Save one. On September 4, 1993, he was scheduled to preach to the Welsh National Convention once again. There would be well over fifteen hundred people there.

He was to preach in a Masonic Temple, the only building suitable to hold the anticipated crowd. The building was full of the kinds of "temple" adornments common to the Masonic organization, but strange to us outsiders. As you might expect by now, he intended to use that setting to his advantage. He would explore the theme of Christ's coming to his earthly and heavenly temples.

By that summer, his kidney was removed, he underwent a second major surgery to remove another unrelated tumor, his body was blasted with radiation countless times, and his veins were filled with all manner of drugs in an effort to halt the angry aggression of the cancer. Then in June 1993, after he suffered a few weeks of sudden uncontrollable wobbling (an indicator that the cancer was compressing his spinal cord) surgeons operated to remove masses of tumors from his spine. They informed us that had the operation been delayed even by a day or two, he would have been paralyzed permanently. As it was, there was real doubt he would ever walk again.

Nonetheless, in the following weeks, he fought to walk. First against a wall, then with a walker, then with a four-point cane, and finally, with a single cane. With a little over a month to go to the convention, my mother came into his room to find him standing. Simply standing. For ten minutes. Standing. Twenty minutes. Standing. And finally, a full thirty minutes. Standing. He was preparing his legs for the demands of that Labor Day sermon.

It was, however, not to be. On August 31, four days before that weekend, having never delivered that temple sermon, he went on to see Christ in his temple.

My father's final sermon consisted simply of standing. In the end, it was a sermon on preaching itself.

A Few Parting Thoughts

Yours is a challenging vocation. But there is tremendous hope and comfort for us all in the word *vocation*. You have been called by *God* to do what you do. Therefore, God will not leave you without appropriate provision for the task. What you lack (and we all do lack), God makes up in other ways.

Plus, you were called by *us* to do what you do. With a few denominational exceptions, we voted to have you come shepherd us. And we heard you preach before you came. So we're on your side here, rooting for your success.

Allow me to state two seemingly contradictory but hopefully comforting things. First, there is no way you can do everything in this book. Second, you *are* doing everything in this book in some fashion or another.

You are choosing texts, creating titles, using your body, articulating with voice and words, wearing clothes, researching the original languages, trying to find ways to make it all interesting and applicable, and on and on.

You didn't magically and immediately know how to do all of the things explored in this book. You have been developing that knowledge base and ability one piece at a time. And you are continually learning, adjusting, improving, and expanding.

This book has taken the various components of preaching and viewed them from the pew, encouraging you to answer the question, "Why do you do the things you do?" It is my hope that this perspective has provided you with additional resources for your journey of preaching with intention.

Your best days of preaching are ahead of you. Go up to that pulpit with joy and the expectation that God, by the power of his Holy Spirit, is going to do great things through your proclamation of his word this Sunday.

But don't carry this book to the pulpit with you. Just take your Bible and let it loose!